The Next Fifty Years
The United Nations and the United States

The Next Fifty Years
The United Nations and the United States

Tom Barry

with Erik Leaver

Resource Center Press
Albuquerque, New Mexico

Published by the Interhemispheric Resource Center

Interhemispheric Resource Center
Box 2178 / Silver City, New Mexico 88062-2178
resourcectr@igc.apc.org

Library of Congress Cataloging-in-Publication Data

Barry, Tom, 1950-
  The next fifty years : the United Nations and the United States /
Tom Barry with Erik Leaver. — 1st ed.
      p. cm.
  Includes bibliographical references and index.
  ISBN 0-911213-61-9
  1. United Nations—United States.   2. United States—Foreign
relations—1993- I. Leaver, Erik, 1971-   . II. Title.
JX1977.2.U5B33 1996   96-14989
341.23'73—dc20   CIP

Acknowledgments

This book is part of a larger project of the Interhemispheric Resource Center (IRC) examining the state of U.S. foreign policy in the post-cold war era and exploring constructive alternatives. Carmen Alicia Nebot, an IRC board member and director of the United Church of Christ's Global Education and Advocacy Program, set this book in motion with her suggestion that the IRC produce educational materials about the role of the United States in the United Nations—an issue of fundamental importance in international affairs.

This book benefited immensely from the comments of Phyllis Bennis, William Durcher, Richard Falk, Victoria Holt, Jim Paul, and Michael Renner. The UN Secretary General's press office and Department of Public Inquiries were extremely helpful in our research work. Generous support for this work was provided by the Sisters of St. Francis and the John D. and Catherine T. MacArthur Foundation.

Contents

Figures

Introduction

Not that long ago most political tendencies accepted that history was moving forward—that there was an inevitability about the progress of human affairs. By fits and starts, albeit with backward slides, it was believed that humankind was finding better ways to govern and care for itself. Socialists and the aptly named progressives of the left were the most ardent believers in the progressive course of history. Liberals, too, championed the conviction that the forces of capitalism and democracy would inevitably establish their supremacy and result in widespread socioeconomic progress.

Today, there are few who would assert their faith in the inevitability of a better tomorrow. The collapse of the Soviet bloc, the failures of revolution, and the monolithic strength of capitalism have shattered the faith of the left that the interests of the poor and working masses would one day triumph over the interests of the few. Liberals have seen communism crumble, political democracy surge, and capitalism establish a global dominion. But there is little sense of where to go from here—this era being what one political analyst called "the end of history." Moreover, this final resting place of history is getting more uncomfortable, owing to widespread social disintegration, rising economic polarization, and the increasing fragility of nation-states. Meanwhile the reactionary right, true to its conservative philosophy, continues to look to the mythical past as a model for the future.

A new world order is emerging in this post-cold war era. This book examines a global entity that must be part of any effort to revive a conviction that people and their governments can and should seek to realize a progressive vision of the future. More than a half century ago, citizen activists and world leaders did look ahead in establishing the United Nations as the caretaker institution of the postwar era. In 1995, events surrounding the UN's 50th anniversary celebrated the organization's longevity and its achievements. Rightly so. The United Nations represented an important step forward in the ordering of international affairs. Its founding was an affirmation that humans can and will find more suitable ways than waging war to settle their differences and improve their conditions. Today, more than ever, it is clear that such an international institution is fundamental to ordering human affairs in a world increasingly integrated by finance, trade, production, communications, immigration flows, and even culture.

The United Nations and the other international institutions established at the close of World War II are, however, due for a critical evaluation if they are to help guide us into the next century. As the global entity charged with maintaining peace and improving human welfare, the United Nations deserves our special attention.

It is now time to project the United Nations into the next fifty years of international relations. Is the structure of the United Nations adequate for the challenges ahead, and what new directions should it pursue in this world so vastly transformed by the forces of globalization? In this time when economic integration is reordering human affairs and when the sovereignty of nation-states is increasingly questioned as the organizing principle of global affairs, this international institution merits renewed attention and consideration.

United Nations in the Era of Globalization

Global politics and economics look considerably different than in the era of Churchill, Stalin, and Roosevelt, when respect for national sovereignty was considered fundamental to world peace and when economic systems were largely national. No longer does Britain hold a claim to global leadership, and the resurgent economic powers of Germany and Japan show no signs of taking leadership positions in global political affairs. The Soviet Union disintegrated—a victim less of the cold war than of its own authoritarianism, dogmatism, economic mismanagement, and military ambitions. The United States no longer approaches international affairs with the confidence and vision it once manifested. The economic and political shortcomings of socialism, as evidenced in the Soviet Union, China, and Cuba, have diminished that system's credibility as an alternative to capitalism.

Capitalism, although itself deeply flawed as an economic system, is now truly global. The international marketplace is reordering the world, and the ideology of economic liberalism dominates political and social thought. Capitalism is no longer nationally based but is instead globally integrated. We live in an increasingly interdependent world in which labor, finance, production, and trade transcend national boundaries. Accompanying this economic globalization is the globalization of communications. New technologies have facilitated information transfer, benefiting the world's leading elite economic actors and opening new possibilities for cooperation among the peoples of the globe.

Photos of earth taken by the space missions of the 1960s and 1970s created a new consciousness about our common condition as residents of this planet. Ecological catastrophes, narcotics flows, the spread of AIDS, and the rising numbers of economic and political refugees have all heightened this awareness. In the past fifty years, business and social organizations have gone global. Corporations are now transnational, and nongovernmental organizations from unions to research institutes have found that a global focus is fundamental to any understanding of today's social, political, and economic conditions. "Global problems need global solutions," concluded Representative James Leach, the codirector of the U.S. Commission on Improving the Effectiveness of the United Nations.

Fifty years is not enough. Certainly there are many problems. The United Nations has fallen short of the universalist goals expressed in its charter and too often has served the narrow objectives of its strongest members. It has been justly criticized for its inefficiency, bureaucratic duplication, and faulty leadership. Nonetheless, it is an institution that should be reformed, not discarded.

If the world is to become a more peaceful and just place, the United Nations must play a central role. This will require a deeper commitment to the United Nations and its principles not only by the constituent states but also by informed and active citizens. Any such renewed commitment will depend on the actions and policies of the United States, which continues to be the most influential member of the United Nations. The enlightened leadership of the United States, whether willing or reluctant, is a critical factor in any successful UN reform. For this reason, this book places special focus on the troubled and controversial relationship between the United Nations and the United States.

The Next Fifty Years: The United Nations and the United States is not intended to add to the avalanche of criticism already falling over the United Nations. Rather we hope the book plays a part in stimulating informed public support for international institutions dedicated to global peace and prosperity. Admittedly, there is currently little political will, especially among U.S. political leaders, for a new commitment to the principles of multilateralism and internationalism, which help define the United Nations. Yet as the United States comes to recognize its own reduced ambition to police the world and to guide global development, the need for a strong international organization will become ever more apparent.

The United Nations is deeply flawed, but it is an indispensable institution—no other organization brings the diversity of world interests together at one table with the idea that all participants are equal. It is important now to gain a better understanding of its past failures and successes, and to put forward some of the reforms that will make it a stronger institution in its next fifty years.

Chapter One

From Versailles to Dumbarton Oaks

Any attempt to reform today's United Nations must contend with the enduring historical roots that still shape the UN's structure and purpose. The origins of such pressing current issues as the composition of the Security Council, the limited role of the General Assembly, the selective character of peacekeeping missions, the dominance of the United States, and the organization's failure to address North-South economic imbalances can all be found in the history of the UN's founding. It is a history driven by the major powers of the northern hemisphere, which on two occasions in the first half of this century had gone to war to determine who would hold the reins of control—political, economic, and military—over the rest of the world.

Even before this century began, there emerged a model for an international organization. It was a world-wide structure not of states, however, but of workers' associations. But like its successors, the First International, established in 1864, never matched the high hopes of its founders. It was not until the cataclysm of trench warfare and the disrupted international trade caused by the First World War that the world's capitalist states began formulating plans for an international organization that could keep the peace and guarantee the flow of international commerce. In the heat of war, the leaders of the allied powers began to consider proposals to restructure international relations in the postwar era.

The United States, which was not so bound to a history of colonialism and mercantile rivalries, took the lead in envisioning a new world order for the twentieth century. As part of his Fourteen Points setting out the U.S. objectives in the war, President Woodrow Wilson in 1918 underlined the need for an institutional framework for collective security, arbitration of disputes, and limitation of armaments. He proposed that a general association of nations be formed "for the purpose of affording mutual guarantees of political independence and territorial integrity to great and small states alike." Wilson's vision of a new international order proved influential at the Versailles Peace Conference of 1919 and sparked the creation of the League of Nations.

Previous to World War I, a system of neutrality and alliances had been designed to protect territorial integrity (and colonial boundaries) and to ensure peace among the world's major powers. The deliberate violation of Belgium's neutrality by Germany at the start of the war highlighted the need for a new system to guarantee international peace. In 1919 the League of Nations was founded on the principle of collective security. In a collective security system, an armed attack by any one state is viewed by the other members as an attack on the international community—broadening the notion of national self-defense to a unified reaction to incidents of aggression. Since the strength of a collective security system depends on such united action, declarations of neutrality only weaken the peacekeeping system.

The League of Nations proved weak and ineffectual, however. The absence of the United States, which failed to ratify the treaty despite the fundamental role of President Wilson in its creation, considerably weakened the power and authority of the League. Bowing to rising isolationist sentiment in the country and reacting to the president's partisan and secretive handling of the League of Nations proposal, the U.S. Congress voted against joining the new international body. This lack of participation by the world's leading economic power doomed the League of Nations to playing a marginal role in the interwar period.

Although the United Nations was founded as a collection of nations, it was also seen as the foundation of a world government.

Although the League did successfully manage several minor disputes, it failed its main test—that of preventing the outbreak of the Second World War. Fueled by fascist rhetoric, aggressive nationalism, and imperial ambitions, the Axis powers of Germany, Italy, and Japan shattered the fragile system of collective security and international trading relations that had emerged following the First World War. Although it was not until 1946 that the League was formally disbanded, it had existed as a hollow shell since the early 1930s. There is little question that the League of Nations represented a grand step forward in humankind's attempt to manage global affairs, but for the colonies and dependencies of the third world the League of Nations was more of a club for the colonial powers than an organization that represented the interests of all the world's populations.

In the throes of World War II, the outlines of another international organization took shape. The Atlantic Charter of 1941, which set out the terms and objectives of U.S. support for Great Britain in the war, referred to the need to establish "the means of dwelling in security." On the first day of 1942, twenty-six nations signed the Declaration of United Nations at Washington, D.C., declaring their intention to remain allies during the war.

The term United Nations became the name of the new international organization planned during a series of meetings in 1944 among world leaders at Dumbarton Oaks in Washington. The UN Charter was prepared by representatives of fifty governments participating at the United Nations Conference in San Francisco in June 1945, where the Charter was signed. It was not, however, until October 24, 1945, that the United Nations was officially established after fifty-one, mostly northern nations had ratified the Charter. The first General Assembly convened in London in January 1946, but the United Nations found a permanent home in New York City. With the exception of the International Court of Justice, the headquarters of the central organs of the UN are found in New York, which has become the diplomatic crossroads of the world.[1] The offices of the UN's associated organizations, however, such as the World Health Organization and the International Labor Organization, are generally not located in New York but in Geneva and elsewhere in the world.

The siting of the UN headquarters in New York reflected the fundamental role played by the United States in establishing the UN and shaping its structure. As the dominant world power, the United States wanted to an institution that would not contest its new hegemonic position. To ensure that its plan for the institution was adopted, the U.S. government mounted a campaign of diplomacy and spying, including the interception and decoding of the communications of its closest allies. According to historian Stephen Schlesinger, who reviewed the classified files of this period, the information acquired clandestinely by U.S. agents helped the United States "to control the debate, to pressure nations to agree to its positions, and to write the UN Charter mostly according to its own blueprint." [2]

As set forward in the UN Charter, the maintenance of international peace and security is the UN's principal goal. The UN's founders, however, did not use the term "collective security," probably because it was associated with the failures of the League of Nations. Other related goals include: developing friendly relations among nations based on respect for the equal rights and self-determination of peoples; cooperating in the solving of international economic, social, cultural, and humanitarian problems; and serving as a center for coordinating efforts to meet these goals.

The United Nations, established at Dumbarton Oaks, was to be the keystone of a new world order of nations joined together not only in a collective security agreement but also as part of a new vision of humanity's common welfare. Although in structure the United Nations was founded as a collection of nations rather than a supranational government, many of its early advocates harbored the hope that the United Nations would eventually serve as the foundation for a system of international governance. Respect for national sovereignty was at the heart of the United Nations, but there was also a recognition that a multilateral accord such as the UN Charter inevitably infringes on the independence and integrity of the nation-state. Today, as economic globalization and a transnational civil society gain force, this tension between national sovereignty and universalism is at the heart of the debate over the UN's future.

For most of its first fifty years, the potential of the United Nations was constrained by the fetters of colonial interests and the cold war.[3] Released from those bipolar tensions, the United Nations rapidly became more involved in solving global problems—not just conflicts between nations but also those within nations. Humanitarian intervention and nationbuilding suddenly became part of the post-cold war agenda. With the world's tragedies broadcast globally by cable news, its people and nations turned to the United Nations for quick remedies.

The United Nations currently finds itself operating in a new era in which geoeconomic objectives overshadow geopolitical ones. It is an era in which the nation-state, the main building block of the United Nations, increasingly finds itself rendered powerless in the face of global forces. "In many ways, the autonomy of states is being superseded by the globalization of capital," observed international law scholar Richard Falk. "This reshaping is demanding and creating a new setting for international law because the traditional thinking cannot cope with the change....In essence, the market has overwhelmed the state, and the situation calls for a reactive, regulatory process." [4]

The collective belief in the necessity of having a global institution such as the United Nations has persisted from Versailles to Dumbarton Oaks and to the end of the cold war. The United Nations, however, is ill-equipped to address the challenges of current global affairs. Burdened by an anachronistic structure and an organizational leadership largely controlled by a few nations, the United Nations lacks the vision, resources, and mandate needed to shape and maintain a more peaceful and just international order.

Chapter Two

A Structural Overview

The end of the cold war and the UN's 50th anniversary have sparked discussion about the appropriateness and effectiveness of the structures of UN institutions. Proposals to reform the structure of the United Nations range from those that advocate an expansion of the organization to allow it to better meet the challenges of globalization to those that call for a radical downsizing or even for its abolition. Clearly, the UN system is due for an overhaul after fifty years. But reform requires strong leadership and a consensus among member nations about the appropriate role for the United Nations in the next century.

Unlike in 1945 when the United States was eager to assume a leadership role in the postwar era, today this country seems willing to lead only when its immediate interests are involved. During the past five decades, the world has changed dramatically, and the United States is no longer the ascendant power it once was. Although having expanded economically, other nations such as Japan, Germany, and China have demonstrated neither a willingness to lead nor the foresight needed to forge an international consensus about what type of global institutions are necessary for the next century. Similarly, the world's less developed nations, once largely united in their call for a New International Economic Order, have put forward no coherent agenda for structural reform of the UN system.

Although deficient in many ways, there is general agreement, with the exception of the extreme right wing, that the organization should be reformed not abolished. A concern of many reformers is that efforts to make the system more representative or more efficient may aggravate existing international tensions and lead to the dissolution or disintegration of this flawed, yet noble experiment in global management.

Principal Organs of the UN System

The United Nations is an evolving system comprising commissions, committees, and specialized agencies (Figure 2a). As new issues arise, such as the need to promote sustainable development, new organizations are created. There is, however, an enduring core of institutions established by the UN Charter that form the main structure of the United Nations. The most prominent of the core institutions are the Security Council, General Assembly, and the Secretariat (headed by the UN secretary-general). Less well-known of the core institutions are the International Court of Justice, the Economic and Social Council, and the Trusteeship Council.

Security Council

The Security Council, the most powerful organ of the United Nations, has as its primary responsibility the maintenance of international peace and security. The fundamental principle underlying this responsibility is that of collective security, meaning that a threat to one nation is regarded as a threat to all. In practice, however, the Security Council has administered a system of selective security, since the permanent members, particularly the United States and the former Soviet Union, often obstructed UN involvement in conflicts in which they were embroiled.

Under the Charter, members have an obligation to submit disputes to the Security Council if they cannot settle them peacefully. The UN Charter authorized the Council to work toward the peaceful settlement of disputes (Chapter VI) and to counter threats to the peace, breaches of peace, and acts of aggression (Chapter VII). Unlike other UN bodies, the Security Council can make decisions that are binding on all members—including the imposition of collective political, economic, and military sanctions.

> **In practice, the Security Council administers a system of selective security.**

Originally, the Security Council had eleven members, five of whom were permanent, namely China, France, the Soviet Union, Great Britain, and the United States. At the close of World War II, these were the victors of the war and their allies. Collectively, they were sometimes called the "Great Powers," despite the great differences of power. In particular, China (at that time represented by the island state of Taiwan) was a much lesser power.[1] A 1965 amendment to the UN Charter increased council membership to fifteen to include the original five permanent members plus ten rotating members. It was specified that these rotating members include three from Africa, two from Latin America, two from Asia, one from

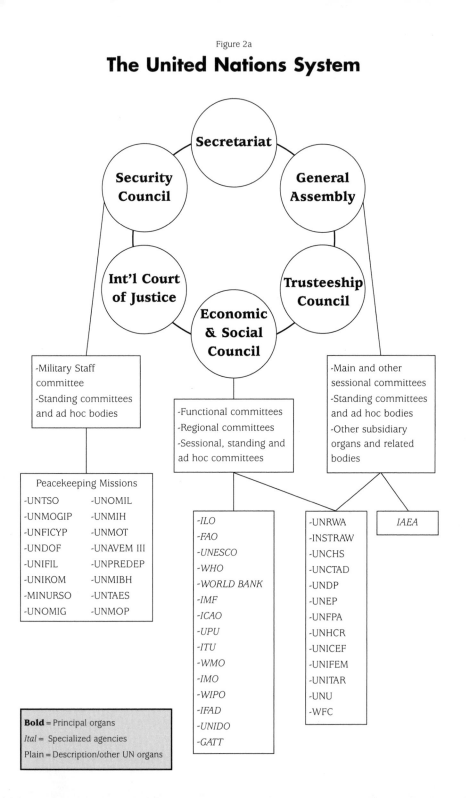

The United Nations System

Secretariat

Security Council

General Assembly

Int'l Court of Justice

Trusteeship Council

Economic & Social Council

-Military Staff committee
-Standing committees and ad hoc bodies

-Functional committees
-Regional committees
-Sessional, standing and ad hoc committees

-Main and other sessional committees
-Standing committees and ad hoc bodies
-Other subsidiary organs and related bodies

Peacekeeping Missions
-UNTSO	-UNOMIL
-UNMOGIP	-UNMIH
-UNFICYP	-UNMOT
-UNDOF	-UNAVEM III
-UNIFIL	-UNPREDEP
-UNIKOM	-UNMIBH
-MINURSO	-UNTAES
-UNOMIG	-UNMOP

-*ILO*
-*FAO*
-*UNESCO*
-*WHO*
-*WORLD BANK*
-*IMF*
-*ICAO*
-*UPU*
-*ITU*
-*WMO*
-*IMO*
-*WIPO*
-*IFAD*
-*UNIDO*
-*GATT*

-UNRWA
-INSTRAW
-UNCHS
-UNCTAD
-UNDP
-UNEP
-UNFPA
-UNHCR
-UNICEF
-UNIFEM
-UNITAR
-UNU
-WFC

IAEA

Bold = Principal organs
Ital = Specialized agencies
Plain = Description/other UN organs

Eastern Europe, and two from Western Europe and other areas.[2] Nonpermanent members, which are approved every two years by the General Assembly, are commonly selected as the result of politicking within the regional groups they represent.

Each member of the Council has one vote. Procedural matters require nine out of the fifteen votes for passage. Decisions on substantive matters require nine votes as well, but a measure cannot pass if opposed by any one of the five permanent members. This is the rule of "Great Power unanimity," or the "veto." All permanent members have resorted to the veto on at least on occasion. If a permanent member does not support a decision but does not wish to block it with a direct veto, it may abstain—a position often favored by China. Other Security Council members can also abstain and have frequently done so for diplomatic reasons.

Objecting to the controlling power given to the five permanent members, the Mexican delegate at the UN's founding conference charged that under the UN Charter, "the mice would be disciplined, but the lions would be free." [3] In theory, the rotating members provide some counterbalance to the permanent members. In practice, however, much of the discussion about policy occurs within the limited circle of permanent members, and due to their inexperience and the pressure exerted by permanent members, the rotating members—called the "temporary ten"—have difficulty wielding any power on the Security Council. More important than the formal or informal discussions among the council members is the military, economic, and political structure of world power, which gives rise to pressures and imperatives that are reflected in council decisions.

The Security Council meets behind closed doors, and its minutes are not available to the public. Its decisions, however, are the ones that achieve the most publicity and have the most immediate impact on global peace. Justice, effectiveness, and longer term legitimacy demand the greater democratization of decisionmaking within the Security Council.

Since 1987, when Premier Mikhail Gorbachev altered the Soviet Union's traditional belligerence to the United States in the United Nations, vetoes have not blocked Security Council action as they did during the cold war. It would be a mistake, however, to assume that the Security Council will never again be stalled by persistent vetoes. China, long accustomed to abstaining in matters that did not directly affect its interests, may one day decide to wield the power of the veto in the Security Council. It is likely that Russia, which assumed the Soviet Union's seat, will once again assert itself as an independent force in international affairs. The declining popularity of Boris Yeltsin and the capitalist reformers make that possibility ever more likely.

Reform of the Security Council is essential if the United Nations is to survive as a credible, effective international institution in the next century. Among the main priorities are its expansion to include permanent members from the South and a permanent seat for Japan. A reconsideration of the European representation on the council—to include a role for Germany—is also important. The phasing out or limitation of the veto will have to be considered.

General Assembly

The General Assembly, which was once hailed as the "parliament of mankind," is the main deliberative organ of the United Nations. Article Four of the UN Charter states that assembly membership is open to states that are "peace-loving," accept the obligations contained in the Charter, and which, in the judgment of the United Nations, have the ability and willingness to carry out the obligations of assembly membership. Members are admitted upon recommendation of the Security Council and approval by the General Assembly. There were only 51 original members of the General Assembly, which by early 1996 had 185 members.[4] Decolonization and the creation of new independent states after the collapse of the Soviet Union were the main factors in the surge in UN membership.

Most of the work of the General Assembly attracts little public attention because of the less sensational matters it addresses.

During the UN's early years, membership petitions were often contested as a result of the rising antagonism between the United States and the Soviet Union. In 1955, however, an agreement was made between these superpowers, and sixteen additional states were admitted. Since then almost all petitions for membership have been accepted with little opposition.[5]

The UN Charter does not specify a minimum population for a country to be admitted as a member. There are at least twelve UN members that have fewer than 200,000 inhabitants. In the General Assembly all members have one seat and one vote. Thus, the ministates have the same voting power as the larger and more powerful states. Proposals have been made to adopt minimum size requirements or to grant proportional representation based either on size or monetary contribution to the United Nations, but diplomats have been unable to overcome the many conflicts and complications presented by these proposals.

The General Assembly opens its 48th session, September 27, 1993.

Assembly members have the right to discuss and make recommendations on all matters within the scope of the Charter. As such, these national representatives are asked to consider a wide range of concerns, including issues of war and peace, world economic problems, problems with colonial rule and basic human rights, nuclear proliferation and environmental degradation, and issues of scientific and technological progress. Although its decisions are not binding on all states, the

General Assembly does pass resolutions that set international norms and formulates new international treaties that have a great moral weight in global affairs. In the early years of the United Nations, the General Assembly played a prominent role in peace and security issues—mainly in the cases of the Korean War and the Suez conflict—because of the inaction of the Security Council. Since then, however, the General Assembly has taken no major role in establishing peacekeeping missions, a role now firmly in the hands of the Security Council.

The General Assembly, which meets annually from mid-September until late December, has six main committees in addition to the plenary. Most issues are delegated to these main committees, which are committees of the whole, although members may decide to address directly some issues in plenary.[6] During every annual session there is an ongoing general debate in which representatives of each government are given the opportunity to address the entire assembly. More than a forum for discussion of pressing peace and security issues, the general debate serves as a platform for national leaders to present their countries' political positions. This debate and most of the work of the General Assembly attract little public attention because of the less sensational matters it addresses (development and health rather than war and peace) and the nonbinding character of General Assembly resolutions about current international affairs.

The General Assembly can be convened in special or emergency sessions for matters of urgent concern. When the Security Council fails to act on a threat to peace because of a veto, the Assembly may be called into session by the Security Council to address the crisis.

Rather than being a world parliament, the General Assembly serves as a forum for international debate. This forum has the potential of being an influential factor in international affairs, as it was in the 1970s when the nonaligned countries offered a new vision for world development. Unlike the Security Council, which reflects the interests of the world's most powerful nations, the General Assembly brings to world affairs the perspectives of the poorer nations of the South, the countries that by their numbers dominate this international forum.

Although overshadowed by the Security Council, the assembly does have the authority to regulate finances and to create new commissions and agencies of the UN system, thereby giving it great influence in such matters as human rights, economic development, public welfare, and environmental conservation. Over the years there has been a notable decline in the influence of the General Assembly. During the cold war, a time when action by the Security Council was often blocked by vetoes, the General Assembly was an important force for decolonization and for a whole range of social and economic issues facing the nonindustrialized world.

In recent years the humanitarian and developmental work of the United Nations has been marginalized by the peacekeeping operations authorized by the Security Council. With the cold war over and the neoliberal formula for development losing credibility, however, there are rising concerns about the global character of developmental, environmental, and human rights issues. Such concerns can be addressed adequately only by the General Assembly as the forum for all the world's nations.

Secretariat

The UN Secretariat, or permanent staff, employs about 15,000 people from more than 150 nations. This includes not only those who work at the UN's main offices in New York and Geneva but also those experts who oversee economic development and peacekeeping projects in the field. In addition, the UN system employs approximately 17,000 people in the specialized agencies. Directing the Secretariat is the UN secretary-general, currently Boutros Boutros-Ghali, who is appointed by the General Assembly upon recommendation by the Security Council. By tradition the secretary-general is appointed every five years but can serve more than one term.

The secretary-general—who has always been male—is assisted by numerous deputies and assistants, who are appointed by the secretary-general often times responding to the recommendations of member nations, particularly the United States.[7] Besides being responsible for the overall administration of the United Nations,

Employees of the Secretariat receive lower salaries and fewer benefits than their counterparts at the World Bank and IMF.

the secretary-general plays an important diplomatic role in world affairs. He can, for example, introduce matters of peace and security to the Security Council. An annual report presented by the secretary-general to the General Assembly is another avenue of influence regarding vital international issues. Assembly members are, however, under no obligation to respond to initiatives proposed by the secretary-general. With respect to the specialized agencies, the secretary-general is the first among equals and has no invested power to coordinate or redirect the work of the agencies of the UN system.

As the United Nations has grown in membership, so has the size of its bureaucracy. Because of the increase of related and overlapping departments and offices, a long-overdue restructuring of the Secretariat was undertaken in 1992 that eliminated numerous offices and consolidated departments. Despite this restructuring, the Secretariat remains the target of criticism for its politicized personnel system and bloated bureaucracy. Although there is certainly much room for improvement, it should be recognized that employees of the Secretariat receive lower salaries and fewer benefits and perks than their counterparts at the World Bank and International Monetary Fund (IMF).[8]

By tradition and practice the secretary-general has to meet with the approval of all the permanent members of the Security Council. For the most part, this has not led to the appointment of leaders of vision and determination. One notable exception was Dag Hammarskjold (1953-61), who won the United Nations a new worldwide respect during his tenure. Boutros Boutros-Ghali, the current secretary-general (appointed in 1992), has been widely criticized for his unrealistically expansive views about peacekeeping, failure to represent third world interests, and subservience to the United States.

Although the Secretariat has been much criticized for having a large, ineffective bureaucracy, the lack of a specialized information unit to inform the secretary-general of conflicts that need UN attention and the absence of a rapid deployment force indicate that an expansion of the

Secretariat may be in order. Such an expansion of functions would improve the secretary-general's ability to help the Security Council respond rapidly to threats to global peace.

Economic and Social Council (ECOSOC)

ECOSOC administers UN activities in the areas of promoting higher living standards, full employment, and development; finding solutions to international economic, social, and health problems; promoting international cultural and educational cooperation; and protecting human rights and fundamental freedoms. These activities are undertaken by five regional economic commissions (including the Economic Commission on Latin America and the Caribbean), functional committees (including the Commission on Human Rights), and an array of subcommissions, working groups, and expert groups all coordinated by ECOSOC. In addition, the many specialized agencies and autonomous organizations of the UN system come under the purview of ECOSOC, which accounts for about 80 percent of the UN's budget.[9]

ECOSOC has 54 members, who are elected by the General Assembly for three-year terms. No government enjoys a permanent seat on ECOSOC, but the five permanent Security Council members are routinely included. Because these Security Council members tend to control ECOSOC, many developing countries prefer to introduce economic development and social issues in the General Assembly where the permanent members exercise less influence. Due to this complication, the General Assembly has created special committees for substantive discussion and action on international economic development matters that duplicate ones created by ECOSOC.

As an institution responsible for international economic and social issues, ECOSOC is largely dysfunctional. It never became the true counterpart to the Security Council in economic and social affairs. Its large membership renders it a cumbersome policymaking body, a problem compounded by the fact that the General Assembly also involves itself in economic and social matters. The fact that the Bretton Woods institutions are functionally outside the UN system has also made it difficult for ECOSOC to coordinate UN development programs.

For many critics, ECOSOC illustrates how the United Nations has failed as a development agency. Although there is little doubt that ECOSOC is an inefficient and ineffectual part of the UN bureaucracy, at least part of its failing is due to its lack of control over the World Bank and IMF and the lack of support among many members for the idea that the United Nations should help guide global economic development. Some suggest that ECOSOC should be regarded simply as another one of the General Assembly's main committees instead of being a principal organ of the UN system. Attempts to reform ECOSOC would undoubtedly raise difficult questions about the proper role of the United Nations in economic matters.

In recent years, peace and security issues have overshadowed development issues. Yet economic globalization and the social polarizing that results from the supremacy of the unregulated international market may soon make such developmental issues as the control over capital flows, debt relief, and a code of conduct for transnational corporations more of a priority in international affairs.

Trusteeship Council

The Trusteeship Council has been responsible for overseeing territories that had formerly been administered by the League of Nations, those voluntarily placed under UN trusteeship, and others that were detached from the Axis powers after World War II. Although territories exist outside the trusteeship of the United Nations, those that have been under direct UN oversight have either obtained their independence or incorporated within other nations.[10] Palau, the sole remaining trust territory, became an independent country in 1994 and was granted membership in the United Nations. Consequently, the Trusteeship Council is at this time essentially a nonperforming division of the United Nations.

By the mid-1990s the question about what to do with "failed states" became part of the discussion about the future of the United Nations.

European nations initially feared that the U.S. plan for a trusteeship council was to challenge the colonial empires of its allies. The Trusteeship Council, however, was not established to promote decolonizaton following the postwar era. British Foreign Secretary Anthony Eden noted that the purpose of the council was mainly to allow the United States to acquire control of Japan's territories in the Pacific and that the "system is not to be applied to any region in Europe nor to any colonies belonging to the Allied countries." [11]

Ironically, at the very time when the United Nations has ended its trusteeship responsibilities, it has been suggested that new territories be placed under UN supervision. During the UN's first fifty years, the emphasis was on decolonization and self-determination of peoples. By the mid-1990s, however, the question about what to do with "failed states" became part of the discussion about the future of the United Nations.

As part of the new *realpolitik* approach to global affairs, it has been proposed that the United Nations take over the responsibility for administration of territories and nationbuilding in those areas where there is no regional power, such as the United States or Russia, to play a leading role. Such proposals are criticized by many of the less developed nations as giving too much power to the United Nations and regional hegemons to intervene in what are essentially domestic affairs. Before such an expansion of the trusteeship responsibilities of the United Nations occurs, reforms are needed to ensure that the UN is truly a global institution and not one that responds only to interests of the most powerful nations.

International Court of Justice

The International Court of Justice, commonly referred to as the World Court, was established after the Versailles Treaty of 1919 and was later incorporated into the UN system. The court's main function is to hear legal disputes between members, although the World Court also renders advisory opinions about the legality of the work of UN agencies themselves. The location of the World Court at The Hague in the Netherlands helps isolate its judges from the political disputes and pressures that swirl around the New York City headquarters.

The power of the World Court has been diluted by domestic legislation limiting the court's jurisdiction and by the failure of nations to honor court decisions. Nonetheless, the court has been more active in recent years, an indicator of the increasing international connections arising from changing patterns of world trade, finance, investment, and communications.

The World Court is responsible for upholding the "rule of law" in international relations. As it is, however, nations can simply ignore unfavorable rulings. The United States is the court's most notorious outlaw. The Reagan administration, after receiving favorable rulings concerning the Iranian hostage crisis and a Canadian fishing-rights dispute, withdrew from the court when Nicaragua successfully demanded reparations from the United States for its attempts to overthrow the government and destabilize the Nicaraguan economy. In 1988 the United States ignored the court again during deliberations over the legality of the U.S. statute ordering the Palestine Liberation Organization to close its UN mission in New York.[12] The World Court could play a fundamental role in maintaining international law as well as promoting global peace, security, and development if all the world's nations would commit to abide by its decisions, even when unfavorable.

System of Agencies

The United Nations is often judged on the success or failure of its peace operations. Commonly overlooked in assessments of UN achievements is what collectively could be called its development, humanitarian, and regulatory agenda. This is the work carried out by its specialized agencies, which are funded separately from the UN's regular budget. The UN's international conventions or treaties must also be considered a key component of its development agenda.

A narrow evaluation based strictly on the effectiveness of the Security Council and the secretary-general in ensuring international peace and security also overlooks the UN's critical role in the areas of nuclear nonproliferation and disarmament through the UN-affiliated International Atomic Energy Agency (IAEA) and the Conference on Disarmament. Without the UN system, the Nuclear Non-Proliferation Treaty (NPT), Biological and Toxin Weapons Convention, and the Chemical Weapons Convention may not have been possible.

The Fourth UN International Conference on Women in September 1995 was another reminder of the fact that it is the United Nations that has been largely responsible for placing pressing social issues about women, children, population, poverty, and human rights on the international agenda.

In evaluating the United Nations, it should also be remembered that the UN environmental conference in Stockholm in 1972 made global ecology an international issue just as it was the UN's Earth Summit in 1992 that made the term sustainable development part of the international language of development. Not only have these conferences helped redefine and focus new attention on global development issues, but they have led to the signing of international conventions that help ensure that children's rights are respected, endangered species are not traded, and Antarctica is protected from mining operations.

As part of the generalized assault on the public sector, this "soft" side of the United Nations has come under attack by those who believe that development is best managed by the private sector and that the UN's development agencies are inefficient and corrupt. During the Reagan administration, the U.S. government joined the right wing in an ideological assault on UN agencies for their leftist, anti-U.S. tendencies. They charged that UN agencies should be focused on promoting international trade and investment and on protecting intellectual property rights rather than on establishing codes of conduct for transnational corporations and fostering a new international economic order.

Just as the UN's main organs are ripe for reform, so too do the multitude of UN agencies need serious review. Better coordination is necessary as is the streamlining of many agencies. In the search for peace and security, however, the fundamental importance of equitable and sustainable development must be recognized. Better accounting and accountability

The UN's international conventions must be considered a key component of its development agenda.

are certainly part of what is lacking. Other elements of a reform package include improved coordination between UN and government programs, more NGO participation, and a substantial reduction in the autonomy of the World Bank, IMF, and World Trade Organization (WTO).

Described here are several of the more important specialized and autonomous agencies and organizations that form part of the UN system. These institutions, known as the UN's specialized agencies, commonly have their own boards of directors and budgets, although they are linked to the United Nations through administrative and funding agreements. These agreements usually establish a flow of information between the agency and the United Nations and set ground rules for UN interactions with and recommendations to the agencies. Not included in the list are many other agencies that also provide substantial contributions to global welfare such as the UN Population Fund (UNFPA), which has promoted family planning in more than one hundred countries, and the International Civil Aviation Organization (ICAO), which has helped increase the safety of world air traffic.

Food and Agriculture Organization (FAO)

The FAO was founded to raise levels of nutrition and standards of living, to secure improvements in the efficiency of production and distribution of all food and agricultural products, and to better the condition of rural populations. The FAO gathers and distributes information relating to nutrition, food, and agriculture. It also provides technical assistance to member nations and can make national and international recommendations regarding research, education, conservation, processing, marketing, and distribution of food and agricultural products. The organization has met deserved criticism for contributing to the demise of small farming and the increase in food insecurity because of its enthusiastic support for the Green Revolution, agrochemicals, and agribusiness techniques over the traditions of family farming. A biennial conference, to which all FAO members are invited, is the institution's policymaking body, while a council of approximately fifty representatives serves as its administrative arm. Critics hope that the departure of Edouward Saouma, FAO's director of eighteen years, will open the FAO to reform and a more environmental and people-friendly approach to agricultural development.

General Agreement on Tariffs and Trade (GATT)/World Trade Organization (WTO)

In much the same way that the IMF and the World Bank are members of the UN system but maintain their independence, so too have GATT (established in 1947) and the WTO (its successor organization) functioned. The WTO, which superseded GATT in 1995, is a multilateral organization that works to reduce barriers to international trade. It is formally considered an autonomous, affiliated organization of the UN system, although it is actually completely independent.

International Atomic Energy Agency (IAEA)

The International Atomic Energy Agency's basic goals are "to seek to accelerate and enlarge the contribution of atomic energy to peace, health, and prosperity throughout the world," and to "ensure, so far as it is able, that assistance provided by it, or at its request, or under its supervision or control, is not used in such a way as to further any military purpose." To meet this objective, the IAEA encourages and assists research, development, and practical application of atomic energy for peaceful uses, and attempts to establish and administer safeguards over nuclear materials. Historically a strong advocate of nuclear energy, the IAEA has increasingly had to face the radioactive dangers posed by nuclear plants, particularly those in the former Soviet Union. In many ways, the

IAEA has represented the interests of those nations that have nuclear weapons and do not wish that other nations develop a nuclear military capacity. In its mission to verify that nuclear materials are not diverted from peaceful uses to nuclear weapons or to other nuclear explosive devices, the IAEA has focused more on nations such a Iraq and North Korea than on such U.S. allies as Israel and Pakistan.

International Labor Organization (ILO)

The ILO, established by the Treaty of Versailles in 1919, is the UN agency dedicated to protecting labor standards, improving working conditions, and promoting harmonious industrial relations. Topics addressed by the ILO include forced work, child labor, working conditions of women, workers' compensation, social insurance, minimum wage, occupational safety, migration for employment, and the rights of workers and employers to organize into associations of their own choosing. Its ability to serve as an international agency whose primary purpose is to promote the welfare of workers is undermined by its tripartite character. Each nation is represented not only by the country's labor delegation but also by delegations from government and business. Oftentimes, even the labor delegation falls short of speaking up for the real interests of workers because of the delegation's integration into it's country's foreign policy establishment. Like other UN agencies concerned with the impact of the marketplace on people, the ILO has seen itself marginalized by the ever-expanding influence of the IMF and World Bank.

The United States has a conflictive history in the ILO, though not, as one might expect, because of corporate opposition to ILO positions on international labor standards. Rather, the United States withdrew from the ILO on two occasions in the 1970s due to the AFL-CIO's avid anticommunism, its anti-PLO positions, and its objection to the inclusion of unions in the ILO that were not "free trade unions" like those it represented. In the 1990s, the Republican leadership has targeted the ILO as part of its anti-UN position.

International Monetary Fund (IMF) and the International Bank for Reconstruction and Development (World Bank)

As part of the planning by the major capitalist powers for the postwar period, there was a monetary and financial conference held in July 1944 in Bretton Woods, New Hampshire, which founded the IMF and the World Bank. Three years later, in September 1947, the UN General Assembly approved agreements between the UN

The IMF and World Bank are the two most powerful agencies of the UN system and are the two that are most independent of UN Influence.

and the two Bretton Woods institutions that established the IMF and World Bank as specialized agencies of the United Nations while at the same time recognizing them as independent international agencies. The IMF and World Bank are the two most powerful agencies of the UN system and the two that are most independent of UN influence. Neither institution takes policy directions from the United Nations, but both do submit annual reports to it.

The IMF works as a Federal Reserve System for the world. It uses its resources to buy and sell world currencies and to make loans to assist countries suffering from balance-of-payments problems. The World Bank comprises four institutions: the International Bank for Reconstruction and Development (IBRD); the International Development Association (IDA), the International Finance Corporation (IFC), and the Multilateral Investment Guarantee Agency (MIGA). The IBRD makes loans for infrastructure and development projects at low market rates of interest to less developed countries. The IDA provides long-term loans at low rates of interest to poor countries that cannot meet standard World Bank repayment schedules. The IFC provides risk capital for private enterprise, and MIGA provides risk insurance for private investment.

Since the 1980s both the IMF and World Bank have come under sharp criticism for conditioning their support on the implementation of neoliberal restructuring of the recipient country's economy. Driving this emphasis on structural adjustment is the concern of the IMF and World Bank's main contributors that debtor nations adopt economic policies that will ensure the continued flow of debt payments. A striking feature of both institutions is that, although they were established to maintain and promote global capitalism, they do not meddle in the domestic affairs of the industrialized nations because of the financial resources and political power these nations maintain.

Office of the UN High Commissioner for Refugees (UNHCR)

The UNHCR has become one of the mostly highly regarded agencies within the UN system under the tenure of High Commissioner Sadako Ogata. Its enhanced reputation comes at a time when the number of refugees is rising rapidly. In 1995 there were some 20 million refugees living outside their home countries—three times the number in 1980—along with an additional 25 million people who were internally displaced within their own nations. The recent surge of Rwandan refugees and those from the former Yugoslavia have taxed UNHCR's ability to respond effectively.

Yet while the refugee crisis intensifies and the number of refugees increases, the UNHCR faces a severe budget crisis. The office is further crippled by the practice of earmarking funds for particular programs, thereby hindering the organization's flexibility.

Another concern of the UNHCR is the increasing reluctance of nations, even wealthy ones, to accept refugees. Perhaps the most ominous sign was the U.S. failure to accept Haitian refugees, signifying an abandonment of the principle of "first asylum" by which refugees have a right to remain in countries in which they first seek asylum.

United Nations Development Program (UNDP)

The UNDP is at the same time one of the least understood and most criticized UN agencies. As the UN's coordinating agency of technical assistance for economic development, the UNDP administers projects carried out by other agencies rather than sponsoring its own pro-

In Afghanistan, land-mine victims learn to walk with artificial limbs.
UNICEF helps provide prostheses and orthopedic services.

jects. The UNDP offers technical assistance to protect the
environment, empower women, eliminate poverty, and
promote jobs. For this reason, few people in developing
countries have had direct dealings with the UNDP.
Although the UNDP is frequently critical of the World
Bank's structural adjustment programs, it regularly provides technical assistance for many bank projects.
Indeed, the U.S. government has conditioned its support

for the UNDP on the agency's willingness to coordinate its programs with those of the World Bank and IMF.

In absolute terms, the United States is UNDP's largest donor, but in GDP per capita terms it ranks seventh. Because of its financial contributions, the U.S. government has been able to shape both the direction of UNDP technical assistance and its economic development philosophy, which in recent years have been very supportive of free trade. The UNDP has gained a new stature within the UN system with the publication of its annual *World Development Report*, which contains the frequently cited Human Development Index and which underlines the need for economic policies that help the world's poor.

United Nations Children's Fund (UNICEF)

Founded in 1945 to provide emergency aid to children of Europe in the aftermath of World War II, UNICEF has become one of the most highly respected of the UN agencies. One of the reasons for UNICEF's good reputation is its capacity to work with governments to improve conditions for children and to protect their fundamental rights.

Every year UNICEF saves the lives of an estimated three million children through its oral rehydration and immunization programs.[13] In 1989, the United Nations General Assembly adopted unanimously the Convention on the Rights of the Child, which guarantees the human rights of children. The Convention on the Rights of the Child is proving to be a key element in the campaign to stop child labor and to provide children with their basic needs. As of January 1996, the Convention had been ratified by 186 countries. The United States has signed but not ratified it.

Since its inception, UNICEF has had four U.S. citizens as its executive director, one of the reasons that the United States accounts for such a high proportion (21 percent in 1994) of the agency's governmental contributions.

World Health Organization (WHO)

The World Health Organization, which predated the founding of the United Nations, has one of the best records of UN agencies, owing largely to its role in the eradication of smallpox. Since its founding, WHO has served as the coordinating authority on international public health work. WHO helps to build strong national health services; attempts to eradicate endemic and other widespread diseases; promotes discussion on population and nutrition; encourages research in health; urges adoption of international standards with respect to food, biological, and pharmaceutical products; and furnishes advice and direct aid to governments in emergencies. The stated goal of WHO is, "the attainment by all the citizens of the world by the year 2000 of a level of health that will permit them to lead a socially and economically productive life."

WHO's reputation among health promoters was undermined in 1988 when its longtime director, Dr. H. Mahler, internationally recognized for his advocacy of primary health care and an essential drug policy, retired. He was replaced with Hiroshi Nakajima, who was appointed less for his qualifications and concerns about public health than through his political connections and the lobbying of the Japanese government.

Involvement of Nongovernmental Organizations

The authority of the United Nations arises from the global system of states rather than being an alternative to that system.[14] It is not a supranational world government but rather a collection of governments each pursuing its own interests. It is not a forum for the world's population but, rather, for its nations. This state-centric character of the United Nations is reflected in its structure. Only representatives from nations can vote, while nongovernmental organizations (NGOs) and political groups are granted only observer or consultative status.

It is often forgotten that it was a determined network of church groups and NGOs that provided the internationalist vision reflected in the UN Charter.

Nongovernmental organizations have, since the origins of the UN, attempted to draw the institution away from its anchoring in national governments. While Franklin Roosevelt is duly credited with providing the diplomatic leadership in the effort to create the United Nations, it is often forgotten that it was a determined network of church groups and NGOs that provided the internationalist vision reflected in the UN Charter. These groups were crucial in turning back neoisolationist sentiment in the United States and in building public support for the new international institution.[15]

As World War II raged, the U.S. peace movement was busy laying the conceptual and practical foundations for what was eventually to become the United Nations. The

League of Nations Association, Women's League for Peace and Justice, Federal Council of Churches, and other nongovernmental organizations kept the concept of a postwar international organization on the public agenda. In 1941, for example, the National Peace Council convened a Conference on World Organization, which was attended by Assistant Secretary of State Adolph Berle. Recognizing the importance of winning NGO and church support for the United Nations, the State Department invited NGO representatives to serve as advisers in the deliberations to establish the world body, and forty-one NGOs participated in the founding conference in 1945.[16]

Although the dominance of the World War II victors in the Security Council and the secondary role of the General Assembly were generally criticized by the NGO community, NGO influence was largely responsible for incorporating universalist, participatory, humanitarian, and human rights sentiments in the UN Charter, thereby modifying the otherwise state-centric character of the new institution. One study of the NGO role in the founding and U.S. approval of the United Nations concluded that in the interwar and immediate postwar periods social forces in the form of civic organizations, churches, and peace groups were "important agents in international affairs" and played a major but now neglected role in "agenda setting and legitimization" of the United Nations.[17]

With the deepening of the cold war and fear generated by the McCarthyism of the 1950s, the peace movement lost its momentum and focus. It was, however, the same coalition of NGOs and churches that was central in pushing forward the new international agenda of disarmament and nuclear nonproliferation. In fact, throughout the UN's first fifty years, NGOs and churches were among it's strongest supporters and successfully countered much of the rightwing propaganda against this global institution.

The Economic and Social Council is authorized by the UN Charter to "make suitable arrangements for consultation with nongovernmental organizations which are concerned with matters within its competence." By the early 1990s nearly one thousand NGOs had been granted consultative status at the United Nations. In 1975 the United Nations Non-Governmental Liaison Service (NGLS) was established to foster greater cooperation between UN agencies and NGOs. The NGLS plays a key role in organizing NGO participation in UN development conferences.

Although given no formal voice within the General Assembly or Security Council, NGOs often exert critical influence in urging UN members to take new measures or adopt new resolutions concerning development, such as the UN's decision to enact a ban on drift-net fishing. It is also widely recognized that NGO participation at UN conferences has been a crucial factor in giving the conferences on children, women, population, society, and environment their agend asetting qualities. Most reformers agree that NGOs should be given a greater formal role within the UN system, arguing that networks that bring government agencies together with NGOs have proved more effective in forging peace agreements and implementing development projects.

As the United Nations moves into its second half-century, NGOs and churches continue to search for ways to become more involved in UN affairs. For example, environmental organizations formed the Earth Summit Watch to monitor the work of the UN's Commission on

Sustainable Development and to ensure that international environmental conventions are respected. Citizen summits that parallel UN conferences—such as the recent ones on environment, social development, and women—have become as influential as the official gatherings of UN and government officials.

The main challenge facing the various NGO sectors (environmental, peace, women's, etc.) will be to join together to construct a new vision and plan for the United Nations. In the same way that the peace movement of the 1930s and 1940s helped lay the foundation for the United Nations, it will be up to the NGOs of the 1990s to set the agenda for reform and innovation for the next century.

Chapter Three

Defining the U.S. Role

Just as Woodrow Wilson was the principal architect of the League of Nations, Franklin Roosevelt was the world leader most involved in the creation of the United Nations. That San Francisco was the site of the UN's founding conference and that New York was selected as its permanent home point to the central role played by the United States in the birth of the United Nations.

Although the United States had become the world's economic leader even before the Second World War, it was not until after the war that it was clearly the capitalist world's hegemonic power. Not only was its economy the world's largest and most dynamic, but it had also developed a massive military-industrial complex during the war. As global leader, the United States was determined to shape a new international organization that would simultaneously help keep the peace and create the international conditions necessary for the expansion of its own power and influence. The United Nations would be the keeper of the postcolonial order and the guardian of the emerging new world order.

The optimistic vision of a postwar order maintained by the victors of the previous war was soon shattered by the deepening tensions between the United States, as leader of the capitalist order, and the Soviet Union, as leader of the communist bloc. The United Nations became an ideological and diplomatic forum for both sides of the cold war. Because of the intensifying superpower rivalry, the tools of peacekeeping and collective security were seldom used.

Without the United Nations, it is unlikely that international political and economic conditions would have proved so propitious for the postwar expansion of U.S. trade and investment overseas. The United States has often been critical of the UN's specialized development agencies, but such UN-associated agencies as the International Labor Organization, the UN High Commissioner for Refugees, and the World Health Organization have contributed to international stability by addressing some of the globe's most explosive social, political, and developmental problems.

To its consternation, the United States did not have the influence within the United Nations that it originally assumed it would have. In the aftermath of the war, the decolonization of large parts of Africa, Asia, and the Caribbean resulted in an influx of new UN members who proved reluctant to accede to U.S. leadership. Nevertheless, the United States was still the world's leading superpower and proved successful in using its influence at the United Nations to derail efforts aimed at constraining the free flow of goods and capital.

Given that the United States was the largest contributor to multilateral institutions and was the acknowledged hegemon of the capitalist world, there was little doubt that the United Nations—as well as the World Bank, GATT, and the IMF—would be used to advance U.S. interests. According to one UN expert, the United States

wanted a body that "would oil the wheels of the r
emergent world order, not one that would tear it down
and build new orders."[1]

Anti-U.S. Sentiment in the United Nations

The view that the United Nations would help maintain
the status quo of the capitalist world order was not one
shared by all its members. During the UN's first fifty
years, the U.S. hegemonic position in the institution
came under attack as part of the East-West and South-
North contests for international power and wealth.
Within the Security Council, the U.S. position was
blocked by a steady stream of Soviet vetoes (101 compared to zero for the United States) in the 1945-65 period. As the world's leading capitalist nation of the
industrialized North, the
United States was also
besieged with criticism by a
rising number of less developed nations regarding the
unjust distribution of global
resources and income.

Beginning in the mid-
1960s, the U.S. failure to control the voting pattern of the
nations of the General Assembly became a constant irritant for the United States. The assembly's positions on
such issues as the U.S. role in Puerto Rico, Cuba, and
Vietnam, as well as the global distribution of wealth,
increasingly put the United States on the defensive,
although its veto threat in the Security Council ensured
that the United Nations could take no decisive action
against U.S. policies. The U.S. Permanent Representative

**In the mid-1960s,
the U.S. failure to
control voting
patterns became a
constant irritant for
the United States.**

to the United Nations, Daniel Patrick Moynihan, appointed by President Ford, called the United Nations a "dangerous place for the United States," while Vernon Walters, his counterpart during the Bush administration, declared, "The UN has become a place where many countries seek to achieve a lynching of the U.S. by resolution."[2]

In the early years of the United Nations, the organization was highly influenced by the United States. For example, between 1946 and 1953 the General Assembly adopted over 800 resolutions. The United States was defeated in less than 3 percent of them, and in no case where important security interests were involved.[3] After 1953, however, U.S. influence began to wane. The rising numbers of colonial territories gaining independence and joining the United Nations combined with the emergence of a more militant third world bloc made it increasingly difficult for the United States to obtain favorable votes in the General Assembly.

The decline of U.S. influence in the General Assembly was paralleled by the increasing coincidence between the Soviet Union's positions and those of the third world. In the early 1980s the voting coincidence between the United States and the majority of the General Assembly dropped below 15 percent while the Soviets coincidence rate was close to 80 percent.[4] This new surge in opposition to U.S. positions was largely a reaction to President Reagan's policy of using financial leverage and coercive diplomacy to assert U.S. policies in the United Nations.

In the mid- to late 1980s the U.S. position once again began to prevail in the General Assembly with the U.S. coincidence rate rising to more than 60 percent. The entry into the United Nations of the newly independent states of the former Soviet Union, all recipients of U.S.

aid, has netted the United States a reliable bloc of allies within the General Assembly (Figure 3a). Israel, the largest recipient of U.S. aid and bolstered by U.S. opposition to a string of UN resolutions condemning Israeli violations of international law, has been Washington's most loyal ally.

Although voting coincidence with the United States has increased since the late 1980s, there is still strong opposition in the General Assembly to U.S. policies that violate international law and disregard multilateral solutions. From 1992 to 1995, annual General Assembly resolutions calling for an end to the U.S. commercial and financial embargo against Cuba passed overwhelmingly, leaving the United States isolated with only a few other countries voting against the resolutions.

Politicizing the United Nations

In the 1965-88 period, the United States increasingly took a defensive posture in the General Assembly rather than exercising leadership. In the U.S. view, the General Assembly and many of the UN's development agencies had become politicized—instead of acting to maintain the postwar order, they had ambitions to radically reform it, particularly with respect to U.S. imperial power and the adverse consequences of the global market.

As a neocolonial power (meaning that its control over third world countries relies more on its economic influence than on the political structures of colonialism), the United States supports the UN commitment to decolonization and self-determination. If challenges to colonial rule and expressions of self-determination take revolutionary form, however, then the United States often resists them. Indeed, Washington believes its military

Highest Voting Coincidence with the United States, 1994

Israel	95%
Georgia	81%
Slovak Republic	80%
Hungary	80%
Czech Republic	79%
Poland	78%
Bulgaria	78%
Albania	78%
Moldova	77%
Slovenia	76%

Source: Bryan T. Johnson, "Most Aid Recipients Vote Against U.S. at U.N.," *Heritage Foundation Report*, April 12, 1995.

interventions and clandestine operations in the less developed countries are benign and justified by the end goal of maintaining the liberal world order and pushing back communist advances. When possible, as in Korea, the United States seeks to construct a multilateral front for its foreign operations, but more often than not it pursued its policies unilaterally.

Ironically, it was a Republican president, George Bush, who advocated a renewal of the U.S. commitment to multilateralism. According to Bush, the Persian Gulf War was about "more than one small country; it is a big idea; a new world order" with "new ways of working with other nations...peaceful settlement of disputes, solidarity against aggression, reduced and controlled arsenals, and just treatment of all peoples."

It was, however, a qualified multilateralism to which the United States was committing itself. Washington still insisted on the right to intervene unilaterally when national interests were allegedly at stake, as in Panama; and the U.S. government still maintained a double standard regarding enforcement of UN resolutions or upholding international law in that transgressions by itself or its allies were regarded as "off limits" for multilateral review. Rather than a guiding principle for the "new world order," this new U.S. commitment to multilateralism was mostly a dressing up of U.S. global hegemony following the cold war. It also represented a new post-cold war politicizing of the United Nations by the United States. Summarizing concern about U.S. control, UN correspondent Phyllis Bennis reported, "There is little question that the large majority of countries of the South, as well as some in the North, would like the UN—a reconfigured UN—to play a large part in the collective defense against Washington's effort to impose a global version of its own neoliberal economic and political system."[5]

Following World War II, the United States had assumed that the United Nations would be an instrument of, not an obstacle to, U.S. international ambitions.

The new multilateralism espoused by President Bush had little to do with a truly multilateral approach to global peace and security issues. It was, instead, an affirmation of U.S. preference for international alliances organized by the United States to respond to perceived or potential threats to U.S. national interests.

Peace Operations and the United States

U.S. policy in regard to peace operations, like much of its post-cold war foreign policy, is not coherent. A renewal of isolationist sentiment, new budget constraints, rising concerns about loss of U.S. sovereignty, a deepening recognition of the financial and political benefits of a multilateral peace force, and the continuing U.S. desire to maintain its hegemonic position are among the factors influencing the multilateral peacekeeping policy of the U.S. government.

Responding to rightwing anti-UN sentiment and eager to reestablish the global image of the United States as the world's hegemon, the Reagan administration declined to pay its UN assessments in full and shamelessly resorted to unilateral military interventions (both direct and clandestine) rather than work through the United Nations to achieve international peace. This U.S. interventionism in such places as Grenada, El Salvador, and Nicaragua represented the reasserting of U.S. hegemony. Unilateral intervention was not a new dimension of U.S. foreign policy. Rather it was the continuation of a long tradition (dating back to the mid-1800s) of U.S. military intervention to ensure that U.S. political and economic interests were protected or bolstered. Leftists and internationalists commonly criticized these interventions as being imperialist operations to protect and perpetuate neocolonial relations throughout the less developed regions. But apologists for U.S. military intervention were apt to justify incursions into such countries as Vietnam, Guatemala, and the Dominican Republic as serving the higher good of defending freedom and democracy from the onslaught of communism. One foreign policy scholar dubbed such intrusions "preemptive imperialism."[6] Over time, the more subtle practice of bolstering allied military governments became more common than direct U.S. military intervention.

Following World War II and the UN's founding, the United States had assumed that the United Nations would be an instrument of, not an obstacle to, U.S. international ambitions. But the Soviet Union's own international ambitions, together with the discontent of the UN's ever-increasing number of less developed nations gave rise to a United Nations that did not share the U.S. global vision. Warming of relations with the Soviet Union in the late 1980s, followed by dissolution of the Soviet bloc and the Persian Gulf War, contributed to a less antagonistic relationship between the United States and the United Nations. As part of his conception of a "new world order," President Bush urged Congress to pay the U.S. dues to the United Nations and called for a more activist role for the multilateral organization.

Having won UN approval for its Desert Storm operation in the Persian Gulf, the Bush administration supported twelve new UN peace operations. The United States increasingly regarded the United Nations as an instrument of its own foreign policy—especially in the area of international peace and security—rather than as a multinational organization that operated independently of U.S. interests. At the same time, however, the United States maintained the right to act unilaterally and in opposition to the United Nations, as it did in Panama, in pursuit of perceived U.S. national interest. The instrumentalist character of U.S. multilateralism was expressed bluntly by President Bush's Under-Secretary of State for International Organizations, John Bolton: "There is no United Nations. There is an international community that occasionally can be led by the only real power left in the world, and that is the United States, when it suits our interest, and when we can get others to go along....When the United States leads, the United Nations will follow. When it suits our interest to do so, we will do so. When it does not suit our interests, we will not." [7]

President Clinton began his administration in 1992 strongly committed to UN peace operations and to a policy of "aggressive multilateralism." But the complexities of maintaining peace and defining a U.S. role in the post-cold war era, compounded by a deepening isolationist sentiment in U.S. domestic politics, soon led Clinton to take a more circumspect and nationalist posture with respect to UN peace operations. The euphoria generated by the U.S. show of military might and resolve during Desert Storm quickly faded, and the U.S. government found itself committed to UN peace operations in many parts of the globe. The bills for UN peace operations initiated during the Bush administration began piling up just as the difficulties of resolving conflicts in such places as the former Yugoslavia, Somalia, and Cambodia were becoming more obvious.

Costs for peacekeeping surged between 1988 and 1994. Once again anti-UN sentiment began to grow among the U.S. public and policymakers, and the Clinton administration, rather than using the presidency to promote his announced policy of "aggressive multilateralism," took the politically expedient course of withdrawing from his former expressions of unconditioned support of the United Nations.

This more conservative posture was reflected in a presidential decision directive (PDD-25) issued in May 1994 that set the conditions for U.S. support for UN peace operations. PDD-25 distanced U.S. policy from previous declarations by the Bush and Clinton administrations that had lent support to a primary role for the United Nations in peacekeeping. PDD-25 represents a rejection of multilateralism and internationalism as guiding principles of U.S. foreign policy in the post-cold war period. Instead, "U.S. interests" and "U.S. national security" were put forward as the principal standards for U.S. support for UN peace operations (Figure 3b). The executive summary of PDD-25 stated that peacekeeping "can be one useful tool to help prevent and resolve conflicts before they pose direct threats to our national security."

PDD-25's specification that an endpoint for U.S. participation be stipulated seemed designed more to obstruct further U.S. participation in UN peace missions than to improve the success of those missions. Positing a deadline, while useful in gaining congressional approval for UN missions, creates an inflexible situation that stands contrary to the patience and determination necessary to ensure the success of a peaceful settlement. Additional U.S. objections to integrating U.S. troops within a UN command and the declaration that the United States will not earmark specific U.S. military units for participation in UN peace missions create added obstacles to building an effective UN peacekeeping capacity.

PDD-25 represents a rejection of multilateralism and internationalism as guiding principles of U.S. foreign policy.

In linking U.S. support for UN peace operations so closely to U.S. interests, PDD-25 marked a new conservatism in U.S. international relations. At least part of this new conservatism arose from a perception that the United States could find itself involved throughout the globe in operations lacking clear goals and action plans. It also represented an attempt to accommodate the rising nationalist and isolationist sentiment in Congress, which rejected all attempts to limit U.S. sovereignty in the name of multilateralism and efforts to involve U.S. troops in for-

Figure 3b

Criteria for Peace Operations under PDD-25

- Advance U.S. interests.
- Respond to a threat or breach of international peace and security.
- Have clear objectives and an identifiable position within the range of Chapter VI and VII operations.
- Either:

    1) include a condition of cease-fire and consent of parties, or

    2) include a significant threat to international peace and security in a Chapter VII operation.
- Have the means available to accomplish its task.
- Have an unacceptable consequence if inaction is taken.
- Be tied to clear criteria and timeline for ending the operation.

eign lands where the United States had no direct interests. In addition, this cautious declaration about peacekeeping revealed a weakened global leader—one who, instead of laying out a strategy for shaping a new world order, opted to focus on narrow self-interest.

The immediate impact of PDD-25 was to reduce U.S. and UN involvement in peace operations. In the first year after its enactment, the United Nations approved only one new peace operation. The United States blocked requests for new operations in Burundi, Georgia, and Angola. Most serious, perhaps, was the U.S. unwillingness to endorse a mission to Rwanda until it was too late to save tens of thousands of people from the horrors of ethnic violence. A 1995 report by the private National Commission for Economic Conversion and Disarmament concluded that if other countries replicated the restrictive conditions for approving peacekeeping operations it "would sound the death knell for peacekeeping."[8]

Despite the new restrictions on U.S. support of UN peace operations, the U.S. Congress still fails to appropriate the funds needed to cover its arrears for peacekeeping. With escalating arrears, the United States became the top debtor for UN peace operations in the mid-1990s surpassing the Russian Federation. Other issues, such as the placement of U.S. troops under foreign command, the reimbursement by the United Nations for U.S. goods and services used during peace operations, and Defense Department involvement in UN operations without direct congressional approval, also became subjects of hot debate in the U.S. Congress. Not satisfied with the PDD-25 provisions, rightwing critics in the U.S. Congress continued to advocate reduced U.S. participation in UN peace operations. Although it is certainly the case that the United States is the major financial sponsor of UN peace operations, UN critics ignored the fact that outside of U.S.-led, UN-sanctioned operations, such as those in Kuwait, Somalia, and Haiti, the United States contributes relatively few troops to UN peace operations.[9] The United States accounts for less than 5 percent of UN peacekeepers currently deployed, about the same number as Bangladesh.[10]

Double Standards

The United Nations is not a global institution that stands above the nations of the world and regulates international affairs. Rather it is an organization that, while including all but a few nations, is controlled by the permanent members of the Security Council and particularly by the big three—the United States, Britain, and

France—with the United States the dominant member. As such, UN interventions respond not to some universal standard of peace and justice but to the strategic interests of its most powerful members.

It is not the severity of human rights violations or extraterritorial aggression that is evaluated when considering a peace operation but rather the threat that a conflict represents to the international economic and political order. Although the United Nations appeals to the language of its Charter with respect to international peace and security to justify interventions, the real standard has less to do with universal principles than with national interests.

This double standard has been particularly evident in the U.S. defense of the aggressive and illegal actions of Israel. Since its founding, Israel has violated international norms with impunity because of the protection provided by the U.S. veto. Politics rather than principles dictate UN enforcement and sanctions policies. Israel, for example, has never been subjected to the same level of scrutiny for nuclear weapons production as less-favored states such as North Korea and Iraq.

Territorial violations by Iraq sparked a vast military response, but aggression and illegal occupations by U.S. allies such as Morocco (in the Western Sahara), Israel (West Bank, Golan Heights, Lebanon, etc.), and Indonesia (East Timor) or by the United States itself (Grenada, Nicaragua, Libya, Panama, and Iraq) are disregarded or even defended. In cases where the United States intervenes militarily, it argues that it is responding to threats to or attacks on either its national interests or U.S. citizens. In the case of Libya, the Reagan administration declared that the U.S. bombing of Libya in April

1986 was justified by alleged Libyan support for terrorist attacks on U.S. citizens abroad. A similar appeal to self-defense was employed in the case of the U.S. attack on Baghdad in June 1993 after revelations of alleged Iraqi government involvement in a plot to assassinate ex-President Bush in Kuwait in April.

Also part of the U.S. double standard is that while it is rhetorically committed to maintaining world peace, it is the world's largest arms dealer—having exported more than $56 billion in arms in the 1989-93 period. Indeed, the five members of the Security Council are among the top six arms exporters. Ranked according to export sales, the world's largest arms dealers are the United States, Russia, Germany, France, Britain, and China.

In pursuit of its own foreign policies, the United States has repeatedly demonstrated a lack of respect for international law and the resolutions of the United Nations. The U.S. failure to respect the judgment in favor of Nicaragua by the World Court in 1986, and its insistence that the Security Council impose sanctions against Libya despite the fact that Libya exhibited willingness to abide by a decision of the World Court (which was at that time reviewing the case) illustrate a lack of respect for multilateralism.

Politics, rather than principle, dictate UN enforcement and sanction policies.

The U.S. veto together with its ability to buy votes in the United Nations permit the United States to continue to uphold this double standard. In the diplomacy preceding the war in the Persian Gulf, the U.S. role as purveyor of votes was quite evident. To win multilateral approval for its military response to the Iraqi invasion of

U.S. Ambassador to the UN Madeleine Albright in the Security Council.

Kuwait, the United States opened wide its diplomatic bag of carrots and sticks. To win Egypt's support, the United States offered $7 billion in debt relief. Several less developed countries on the Security Council, including Colombia, Ethiopia, and Zaire, were offered new aid packages, access to World Bank credits, and rearrangements of IMF loans and grants.

In return for not opposing the United States, China was freed from the pariah status into which it had been cast after the repression at Tiananmen Square. A week after China abstained on the Iraqi resolution—rather than using its veto—the World Bank announced that China would be given access to $114 million in economic aid. In contrast, three days after Yemen (one of the poorest countries in the Gulf region) opposed the resolution, the United States cut its $70 million aid package. Minutes after the vote, a U.S. representative was heard telling the Yemeni representative, "that will be the most expensive vote you ever cast."[11]

Money Matters

Accounting for 25 percent of the UN's regular budget, the United States is the largest source of UN regular funds. It is followed by Japan, which contributes 14 percent of the UN regular budget. The United States is also the largest contributor to most of the UN's specialized agencies, although the proportion of its contributions vary greatly.

The United States, the largest contributor to the United Nations, is also its largest debtor. U.S. arrears to the UN are the result of both ideological and budgetary pressures at home. In the early 1980s during the Reagan administration, the U.S. Congress began withholding funds for UN programs and activities of which it did not approve. Included among the programs targeted by Congress were the Special Unit on Palestinian Rights, and projects thought to be benefiting the Palestine Liberation Organization (PLO) and the South West Africa People's Organization (SWAPO). The U.S. government has also blocked funds to the UNFPA (because of its presence in China) and has withheld funds for the implementation of the Law of the Sea (because of its regulation of the activities of mining corporations).

The Reagan administration initiated the practice of withholding a portion of its UN dues to pressure the United Nations to reform its budgetary and staffing practices. Congress authorized the president to withhold 20 percent of the funds in had allocated for the UN and its agencies if those institutions did not take into account the concerns of their major financial contributors. This practice has continued into the Clinton administration, which withheld 20 percent of the U.S. contribution to the UN's regular budget pending the outcome of the UN's

1996-97 budget planning process. The Reagan administration also began the practice of delaying payments on its annual assessments (due every February) until the beginning of the next U.S. fiscal year in October, putting the United States nine months behind in its payments and thereby worsening the UN's liquidity crisis.

Responding favorably to UN budgetary and staffing reforms, the U.S. government in 1992 promised to pay all its arrears by 1997. However, a new wave of anti-UN sentiment in Congress in the mid-1990s when combined with the Clinton administration's own efforts to reduce the budget deficit make it unlikely that this goal will be met. Neither the administration nor Congress included funds for the payments of UN arrears in their consideration of the 1996 budget. As a result, the United States will likely remain the UN's largest debtor nation.

Payment of peacekeeping assessments has been one of the most contentious issues of UN funding in the U.S. Congress. In 1989, when the cost of UN peace operations was increasing and the U.S. assessment had increased by one percent because of the breakup of the Soviet Union, the U.S. government declared that it would no longer pay all of its assessed dues for peacekeeping. Continuing this sentiment, the Clinton administration informed the Secretariat that beginning in 1996 it would pay no more than 25 percent of the cost of UN-led peacekeeping missions—not the 30 percent it had been paying.[12]

Closely related to the intensifying Republican opposition to multilateral peacekeeping were congressional proposals in 1994-95 to reduce U.S. contributions to UN peace operations on the grounds that the United States incurs high peacekeeping costs apart from UN-led operations. Under the Republican-sponsored National

Security Revitalization Act, the U.S. government would unilaterally decide to subtract unreimbursed contributions to peacekeeping from its annual assessment. It is true that the United States is not reimbursed for many in-kind services, such as food aid and logistical support, to UN peace missions. But the United States is hardly alone in this regard, and many of the operations undertaken by the United States, such as those in Haiti and Iraq, were initiated and controlled by Washington. Reimbursing the legitimate in-kind contributions by all countries would aggravate the UN's already severe financial crisis and require the United Nations to raise its assessments on all member states.[13]

Congressional opponents of the United Nations have hindered attempts by the Bush and Clinton administrations to pay off peacekeeping arrears. In keeping with the commitments expressed in the Republican "Contract with America," the Republican Congress in 1995 blocked the administration's proposal to pass on some peacekeeping costs to the Pentagon. It did agree to a plan under which the United States would pay off its arrears at the annual rate of $200 million, but not before exacting new promises that the administration would push for UN downsizing and reconsider U.S. membership in such UN agencies as UNIDO, UNCTAD, the FAO, and the ILO.[14]

A new wave of anti-UN sentiment in Congress makes it unlikely that U.S. arrears will be paid by 1997.

Concerns about the cost of the United Nations should be kept in perspective. The total cost of U.S. assessments and voluntary contributions to the UN system constitute only 0.1 percent of the national budget and represent just 0.7 percent of the U.S. defense budget.[15] Rather than a burden, the cost of maintaining the UN system for the U.S. government and taxpayer could be considered a bargain. At the cost of $7 per U.S. taxpayer, the UN system provides an array of global services—from formulating international conventions and distributing vaccines to deploying blue-helmeted peacekeepers. The 1995 peacekeeping assessments of $3.3 billion was just 30 percent more than the annual budget of the New York City Police Department.[16]

The Public Debate

Just as World War I had sparked clashes between those eager to recognize the new international role of the United States and those wanting to isolate the United States from global politics and economic pressures, so too did World War II stir up new waves of internationalism and isolationism. Today, once again, there is intense debate about the direction the United States should take—whether to embrace the new global order or to define more narrowly the nation's own interests and strengths, whether to accept multilateralism as a principle of conducting global affairs or to rely primarily on unilateral approaches.

Unlike after World War I when the U.S. Congress rejected the League of Nations, internationalism won out over isolationism after World War II. Political and economic leaders recognized that in the ruins of war and colonialism the United States had the opportunity to shape the world according to its designs. With proper direction, this would truly be the American Century. This internationalism, while representing a rejection of isolationism, was not an unqualified endorsement of multilateralism. Multilateral institutions like the United Nations were a convenient vehicle for pursuing U.S. international interests, but the U.S. government certainly did not rule out unilateralism. In fact, the postwar internationalism of the United States chiefly assumed a unilateral character. This camp of internationalists included the free traders, Wilsonian liberals, and the foreign policy establishment.

Paralleling the U.S. hegemonic view, there also emerged an internationalism guided more by moral and political beliefs than by the fortunes of U.S. capital and U.S. geopolitical concerns. Citizen and church groups promoting a just world without war were among the main supporters of the United Nations and deserve much credit for weakening many U.S. citizens' isolationist resolve. Unlike the internationalists linked to the U.S. economic and political power structure, these grassroots internationalists were—and continue to be—more committed on principle to multilateralism and less willing to accept unilateralism as a way to conduct U.S. foreign policy.

U.S. isolationism, fostered by U.S. conservatives, constituted the main domestic political force opposing U.S. participation in the League of Nations and the United Nations. Conservatives, appealing to populist fears of global entanglements, stirred up opposition to multilateral institutions and agreements. Today, sentiment against multilateralism continues to run strong within the right wing but more because of its commitment to unilateralism than due to its isolationism.

In the 1950s and the 1960s, the extreme right wing fanned the anti-UN campaign in the United States with rhetoric asserting that the United Nations and its agencies were part of a communist plot for global control.

Typical of this campaign was the John Birch Society's slogan: "Get the U.S. Out of the UN and Get the UN Out of the U.S." Another slogan that started appearing on car bumpers in the 1960s was, "You Can't Spell Communism Without UN." These strong beliefs did not translate into anti-interventionism, however. As a rule, the anti-UN groups have been strong unilateralists, although at the same time usually harboring the protectionist beliefs of the traditional isolationists. Only within the left has there been a persistent critique of unilateralism, although the postwar politics of "humanitarian" (as in Somalia and the former Yugoslavia) and "democracy" (as in Haiti) interventions have shaken the anti-interventionist principles of many within the U.S. left.

Anti-UN sentiments in the United States have come in waves, fueled first by the anticommunism of the 1950s and 1960s, surging again in the 1970s in reaction to the anti-imperialism of the advocates of the New International Economic Order, and then rising again as part of the Reagan administration's rightwing agenda. In the 1990s, the Gingrich Republicans and rightwing militants resurrected the vilification campaign against the United Nations. The blue helmets of UN peacekeepers replaced the red menace, and the multilateralism of U.S. liberalism replaced communism in the eyes of rightwing militants as the main threats to the United States. The most extreme on the right would abolish the United Nations, regarding it as a supranational conspiracy. Rightwing populists like Pat Buchanan will tolerate no breach of U.S. sovereignty in the name of multilateralism. "A world without the United Nations would be a better world," according to Heritage Foundation research director Burton Yale Pines.[17]

In opposition to the internationalists are the isolationists and the uncompromising nationalists. On the left are those who are skeptical of U.S. global ambitions, having seen the death and destabilization that accompanies U.S. interventions—whether unilateral or behind a multilateral shield—"to make the world safe for democracy." Lately, however, it has been the right wing, led by the Heritage Foundation and other conservative institutes, that has dominated this side of the debate.

Today, the same two sets of internationalists—the capital- and state-centered ones on one side and the people-centered ones on the other—remain the strongest proponents of the United Nations. Both groups counter the criticisms of rightwing and leftwing isolationists and protectionists with arguments to the effect that an integrated globe needs effective global institutions. The difference between the two sets of internationalists is that while those more closely linked to the political and economic power structure see internationalism and multilateralism as the best way to pursue U.S. national interests, those who are more people-centered harbor a vision of international organizations and movements that respond primarily to global priorities rather than strictly national ones.

The real extent of U.S. hegemony and its willingness to take a leadership role has come into question in recent years.

While decidedly not isolationist, the power-structure internationalists are committed to multilateralism mostly as a foreign policy instrument rather than as a principle of international affairs. While multilateral agreements and operations are regarded as preferable, the establishment internationalists are not opposed to unilateralism. The second internationalist camp encompasses many of the citizen and church groups that originally lobbied for the UN's creation together with a newly emerging but still loosely formed coalition of academics, fair trade activists, unionists, and environmentalists who assert that peace, justice, and sustainability are possible only through global organization. Multilateralism is generally synonymous with their internationalism.

One of the key issues regarding the UN's future is the role of U.S. global leadership. During the cold war, both superpowers sought to keep the world's countries, organizations, and movements marching under their respective banners of socialism and capitalism. The disintegration of the Soviet Union left the United States as the only remaining global hegemon. Yet the real extent of U.S. hegemony and the willingness of the United States to continue to take a leadership role in global economic and political affairs have come into question in recent years. Clearly, as amply demonstrated by the Persian Gulf War, the United States remains the globe's only major military power, but its declining economic fortunes together with its increased unwillingness to assume political responsibility for the state of global capitalism have created a leadership vacuum. At this time, no one nation or coalition of nations appears willing to fill this leadership gap.

The paradox of the post-cold war and pre-new world order is that the world has no other leader but the United States—which itself does not have a clear vision of its own future, let alone of a new global order. What is more, much of the international community has grave reservations about following a U.S. leadership that for so long has been characterized by its use of double standards and its pursuit of narrow self-interests.

Addressing this question, Paul Miller, a U.S. citizen sharing his opinion with the United States Commission on Improving the Effectiveness of the United Nations, said: "I agree that nations ultimately act in their own self-interests. The United Nations can be one form of education for all nations, including the United States, as to what is their true self-interest, and the United States can lead the United Nations by means other than military, such as by more exemplary conduct in such fields as the environment, free trade, and human rights. In the long run, this form of U.S. leadership is a key way we can improve the effectiveness of the United Nations."

As the world's military giant and its largest economy, the United States should certainly assume a leading role in shaping the political and economic landscape of the future. Without its leadership and support, such necessary measures as the reduction of the conventional arms trade and controls on transnational corporations will never gain acceptance. Within the United Nations, at least, there can be no serious new operation undertaken or new direction selected without the cooperation, financing, and leadership of the United States. As the public debate continues about the appropriate role of the United States in the United Nations, U.S. citizens face a special responsibility. The United States was the main force behind the creation of the United Nations; and after fifty years this nation, although weakened, is still in the position of having the power to shape the directions, decisions, and even the structure of the world body. Through their voices and actions, U.S. citizens can help ensure that this power is used responsibly in the true interests of all the world's peoples and nations.

Chapter Four

Keeping the Peace

The peacekeeping role of the United Nations elicits both strong criticism and wide support. To "save succeeding generations from the scourge of war" was the primary goal of the founders of the United Nations in the aftermath of World War II. But as a report by the Council for a Livable World Education Fund pointed out, "Despite the hopes of the UN's founders, over 23 million people have died in wars and conflicts since 1945, many the victims of crises which the United Nations did not mediate (or could not resolve)." [1] Nevertheless, the United Nations is rightfully credited for peacefully ending several conflicts and saving many lives.

During the cold war, the peace and security functions of the United Nations were obstructed by the tensions between the communist bloc nations and the leading capitalist nations. The areas of interest defined by the colonial powers on the Security Council also limited the purview of UN peacekeeping. Between 1945 and 1996, members of the UN Security Council vetoed 239 measures involving matters of international security (Figure 4a). Although the cold war stand-off and the veto power of the five permanent members limited UN involvement in many conflicts, such as the Vietnam War, the United

Changing Patterns in Use of Vetoes

Period	China	France	Britain	U.S.	USSR	TOTAL
1946-55	1	2	—	—	75	78
1956-65	—	2	3	—	26	31
1966-75	2	2	10	12	7	33
1976-87	—	10	16	44	6	76
1988-92	—	2	3	13	—	18
1993-95	—	—	—	1	2	3
Total	**3**	**18**	**32**	**70**	**116**	**239**

Source: U.S. Mission to the UN, *List of Vetoes Cast in Public Meetings of the Security Council*, Reference and Research Unit, May 18, 1995.

Nations deserves at least part of the credit for keeping the cold war from breaking out into a world war.

With the end of the cold war and the bipolar global power structure, a new consensus about international security issues and the need for international peace-keepers emerged. The stalemate in the Security Council ended, and only twenty-one vetoes have been cast in the 1988-95 period. During its first forty-three years, the United Nations approved only thirteen peace operations. Between 1988 and 1995, however, the world body approved another twenty-five missions, including the three largest in UN history, in Cambodia, the former Yugoslavia, and Somalia (Figure 4b). By 1996 the United Nations had approved a total of forty peace operations— sixteen of which were ongoing. As of August 1995, there were 68,894 peacekeeping personnel (including 3,254 U.S. troops) in the field at an annual cost of $3.3 billion in 1995.[2] The UN enthusiasm for new peace missions had apparently crested by 1995, however, replaced by an increasing disinclination to sponsor new peacekeeping efforts. The failures of the UN missions in Somalia and Bosnia contributed to this declining enthusiasm for UN peace operations, which was especially evident in the United States, where the Clinton administration had backed away from its initial commitment to multilateralism. In the immediate future, a new surge in UN peacekeeping is unlikely. Conflicts that do not threaten the political and economic order as defined by the world's most powerful nations will be ignored, while the peacekeeping that does occur will be carried out by the major powers, probably with the blessing of a weakened United Nations.

The UN's peacekeeping operations have a mixed reputation. On the one hand, peacekeeping operations have gained respect for their critical role in decolonization efforts, maintaining cease-fires, protecting refugees, and mediating conflicts. On the other hand, they

The failures of the UN missions in Somalia and Bosnia contributed to this declining enthusiasm for UN peace operations.

have been criticized for their tardiness and ineffectiveness and for being controlled by the United States together with the other "Great Powers."

In some quarters, the U.S. use of the United Nations to organize a multilateral response to Iraq's invasion of Kuwait earned the United Nations new respect as an international institution. For others, however, the rush to war and the technological brutality exhibited by the UN-approved response during the Persian Gulf War made a mockery of the UN's commitment to peace. The Security Council, pressured by the United States, opted quickly for war rather than waiting to give diplomacy and economic sanctions a chance. The U.S. domination of the UN-authorized action in the Persian Gulf heightened con-

UN Peace Operations, 1945-April 1996

Mission Name	Start Date . . . . .End Date
UN Truce Supervision Organization	
UNTSO	June 1948 . . . . .Present
UN Military Observer Group in India and Pakistan	
UNMOGIP	January 1949 . . . . .Present
First UN Emergency Force	
UNEF I	November 1956 . . . . . . .June 1967
UN Observation Group in Lebanon	
UNOGIL	June 1958 . . .December 1958
UN Operation in the Congo	
ONUC	July 1960 . . . . .June 1964
UN Security Force in West New Guinea	
UNSF	October 1962 . . . . .April 1963
UN Yemen Observation Mission	
UNYOM	July 1963 . . .September 1964
UN Peacekeeping Force in Cyprus	
UNFICYP	March 1964 . . . . .Present
Mission of the Representative of the Secretary General in the Dominican Republic	
DOMREP	May 1965 . . . . .October 1966
UN India-Pakistan Observation Mission	
UNIPOM	September 1965 . . . . . .March 1966
Second UN Emergency Force	
UNEF II	October 1973 . . . . . . .July 1979
UN Disengagement Observer Force	
UNDOF	June 1974 . . . . .Present
UN Interim Force in Lebanon	
UNIFIL	March 1978 . . . . .Present
UN Good Offices Mission in Afghanistan and Pakistan	
UNGOMAP	April 1988 . . . . . .March 1990
UN Iran-Iraq Military Observer Group	
UNIIMOG	August 1988 . . . .February 1991
UN Angola Verification Mission I	
UNAVEM I	January 1989 . . . . . . .June 1991
UN Transition Assistance Group	
UNTAG	April 1989 . . . . . .March 1990
UN Observer Group in Central America	
ONUCA	November 1989 . . . . .January 1992
UN Iraq-Kuwait Observation Mission	
UNIKOM	April 1991 . . . . .Present
UN Observer Mission in El Salvador	
ONUSAL	May 1991 . . . . .May 1995

UN Mission for the Referendum in Western Sahara
MINURSO   April 1991 . . . . .Present
UN Angola Verification Mission II
UNAVEM II   June 1991 . . . .February 1995
UN Advance Mission in Cambodia
UNAMIC   October 1991 . . . . . .March 1992
UN Protection Force
UNPROFOR   February 1992 . . .December 1995
UN Transitional Authority in Cambodia
UNTAC   March 1992 . . .September 1993
UN Operation in Somalia I
UNOSOM I   April 1992 . . . . .April 1993
UN Operation in Mozambique
ONUMOZ   December 1992 . . . . .January 1995
UN Operation in Somalia II
UNOSOM II   May 1993 . . . . . .March 1995
UN Observer Mission Uganda-Rwanda
UNOMUR   June 1993 . . .September 1994
UN Observer Mission in Georgia
UNOMIG   August 1993 . . . . .Present
UN Observer Mission in Liberia
UNOMIL   September 1993 . . . . .Present
UN Mission in Haiti
UNMIH   September 1993 . . . . . . .June 1996[1]
UN Assistance Mission in Rwanda
UNAMIR   October 1993 . . . . . .March 1996
UN Mission of Observers in Tajikistan
UNMOT   December 1994 . . . . .Present
UN Angola Verification Mission III
UNAVEM III   February 1995 . . . . .Present
UN Confidence Restoration Operation in Croatia
UNCRO   April 1995[2] . . .December 1995
UN Preventative Deployment Force in Macedonia
UNPREDEP   April 1995[2] . . . . .Present
UN Mission in Bosnia and Herzegovina
UNMIBH   December 1995 . . . . .Present
UN Transitional Administration for Eastern Slavonia, Baranja,
and Western Sirmium
UNTAES   January 1996 . . . . .Present
UN Mission of Observers in Prevlaka (Croatia)
UNMOP   January 1996 . . . . .Present

---

1. Projected end date.
2. The Security Council voted on March 31, 1995, to divide UNPROFOR into
three operations: UNPROFOR, UNCRO, UNPREDEP.

Source: Council for a Livable World Education Fund, Project on Peacekeeping and
the United Nations, "UN Peacekeeping Operations Past and Present," June 12, 1995;
UN Spokesman's Office, "Current Peace-keeping Operations," February 15, 1996.

cerns that this multilateral institution was in fact an instrument of U.S. foreign policy.

Although peacekeeping is not the only function of the United Nations, the U.S. media and public tend to base their evaluations of the United Nations almost exclusively on its ability to achieve peace and roll back aggression. Since the United Nations was established primarily as an instrument of collective security, this standard of evaluation is not completely unwarranted. Yet the important humanitarian, developmental, and technical work of all the UN special agencies should also be recognized. Any fair evaluation of the United Nations should also acknowledge that the institution is a collection of nations and that its effectiveness is closely related to the resources and mandate it is given.

The United Nations faces a new age of conflict as the result of the end of the cold war. The legacy of colonialism, which arbitrarily established national boundaries that had little to do with preexisting concentrations of ethnic, linguistic, or religious groups, stands in the background of many of the conflicts, although other intergroup conflicts, such as the one in the former Yugoslavia, predate the colonial era. The cold war, while keeping a lid on many conflicts, set the stage for the current surge in global violence by spreading conventional weapons to client regimes.

Writing in *Foreign Affairs*, Joseph Nye concluded that the old world order provided a stability that has now been shattered:

> The Cold War exacerbated a number of third world conflicts, but economic conflicts among the United States, Europe, and Japan were dampened by common concerns about the Soviet military threat. Bitter ethnic divisions were kept under a tight lid by the Soviet pres-

ence in eastern Europe. A number of third world conflicts were averted or shortened when the superpowers feared their clients might drag them too close to the nuclear abyss. The various Arab-Israeli wars, for example, were brief. In fact some experts believe that a stronger Soviet Union would never have allowed its Iraqi client to invade Kuwait.[3]

Humanitarian Intervention

New conflicts have strained the UN's ability to respond with effective peacekeeping forces and these conflicts raise new questions about the appropriateness and effectiveness of UN peacekeeping. In the wake of bipolarism, the United Nations has become more an extension of U.S. foreign policy. It is an institution being pushed by both the left and the right to become more active in resolving conflicts but which has not been given the resources or authority to act decisively.

Origins and History of Peacekeeping Operations

Although not explicitly mandated by the UN's Charter, peace operations have evolved from the broad authority of the United Nations to settle conflicts and to respond to aggression, as established in Chapters VI and VII of the Charter. Chapter VI covers the "Pacific Settlement of Disputes," while Chapter VII covers "Action with Respect to Threats to the Peace, and Acts of Aggression." Chapter VI does not authorize the use of force except for self-defense. If actions not involving armed forces fail or are not appropriate, the Security Council may authorize the use of force "to maintain or restore international peace and security." In most cases, however, the Security Council has not specified under which chapter it is authorizing or approving a peace operation. In some cases, such as in the Congo in the 1960s, the distinction between peacekeeping and peace enforcement becomes blurred.

The founders of the United Nations did not specify the character or composition of UN peacekeeping forces. Peacekeeping is not even mentioned in the Charter. The founders did, however, establish a Military Staff Committee as the command of the national forces that would presumably be put at the UN's disposal in the event of a conflict. The idea was to mount a collective defense against aggression rather than to serve as a neutral presence in a conflict between two belligerent forces. Under Article 43 of the UN Charter, member states are expected "to make available to the Security Council, on its call...armed forces, assistance and facilities, including rights of passage, necessary for the purpose of maintaining international peace and security." Before the cold war deepened, the "Great Powers" that emerged after World War II had assumed that the United Nations would be able to deploy as many as two million troops that would be available from member nations. In part because of the cold war and in part because of national reluctance to act multilaterally in military affairs, the Military Staff Committee never functioned (other than pro forma meetings), and the UN army was never established.

Terms of Peace

In the UN's lexicon, *peace operations* is a term that refers to a wide range of activities designed to prevent or end conflicts. As described below, there is a broad range of peace operations, which are sometimes divided into two major categories: peacekeeping and peace enforcement. Unlike peacekeeping missions, peace enforcement operations explicitly involve taking military measures to turn back an aggressor or violator of the peace. With respect to the UN Charter, as noted above, the peacekeeping or nonmilitary missions are covered by the provisions of Chapter VI, and peace enforcement missions fall under Chapter VII.

Peacebuilding includes such activities as strengthening government institutions, monitoring human rights, and reintegrating former combatants into the country's economy.

The character and dimensions of UN peacekeeping are not strictly defined by the UN Charter or any other UN document. From the days of monitoring cease-fire lines with a handful of soldiers, UN peacekeeping has become more complex. Not only do the UN peace operations keep the peace, they also often involve a wide range of activities and agencies with humanitarian, developmental, disarmament, and human rights objectives. The increasing complexity of UN peace missions has made them more vulnerable to criticism. Although these new multidimensioned missions have sometimes been too ambitious or not well-coordinated, the broadening of UN peacekeeping beyond cease-fire monitoring has in general been positive. It has resulted from a recognition that an enduring peace may require more than just monitoring a cease-fire line.

The peace operations that are either undertaken by the secretary-general or explicitly authorized by the Security Council range from preventive diplomacy to warmaking.[4] According to Secretary General Boutros-Ghali's 1992 report, *An Agenda for Peace*, "Preventive diplomacy requires measures to create confidence; it needs early warning based on information gathering and informal or formal fact-finding; it may also involve preventive deployment and in some situations demilitarized zones." [5] In addition, the United Nations sometimes attempts to resolve conflicts by mediating peace negotiations between hostile parties.

Frequently, this conflict resolution or peacemaking function of the United Nations, usually managed by civilians, is accompanied by a peace operation involving the blue-helmeted troops deployed under the UN banner. Such peace operations involve the intervention of neutral UN armed forces to ensure that conflictive parties do not resume fighting. They commonly involve truce-monitoring and increasingly include election-monitoring operations, sometimes categorized as observation operations.

The peace operations of the United Nations usually count on the consent of warring parties, but recently in the civil conflicts in Somalia and Bosnia this has not been the case. In both cases, peacekeeping has led to military missions, led by the United States in the case of Somalia and by North Atlantic Treaty Organization (NATO) in the case of Bosnia. The peacekeeping mission in the Congo in 1960 also led to a peace enforcement mission in which UN troops went into combat. The two major warmaking missions authorized, but not directed, by the United Nations were the U.S.-led military campaigns against North Korea and Iraq.

Peace operations increasingly encompass a variation of peacekeeping called peacebuilding. According to Secretary General Boutros-Ghali, the objective of peacebuilding is "to identify and support structures which will tend to strengthen and solidify peace in order to avoid a relapse into conflict." With the involvement of the United Nations in more civil conflict, peacebuilding, sometimes also called nationbuilding, includes such activities as strengthening government institutions, monitoring human rights, managing and monitoring elections, and reintegrating former combatants into the country's economy. "Preventive diplomacy is to avoid a crisis; post-conflict peacebuilding is to prevent a recurrence," explained Boutros-Ghali in his *Agenda for Peace*.

Cold war tensions limited the UN's peacekeeping functions, but during the 1945-90 period the range of UN peace operations did become established. Of the thirteen operations initiated during this period, five were still in operation as of early-1996.[6]

The first peace operation, established in Palestine in 1948, was an observer mission sent to monitor the mediation process. Two years later the UN Security Council (with the Soviet Union absent) gave the United States permission to organize a nominally multilateral force (virtually all U.S. and South Korean troops) to enter into combat against North Korean and allied troops. Although operating under the authority of the United Nations, the use of force against North Korea was not a UN peace operation. It did, however, set a precedent for UN-approved peace operations organized by regional organizations and individual nations.

It was not until 1956 that a UN-directed multilateral peacekeeping force was authorized. The 1956-67 United Nations Emergency Force brought the troops of nations not directly involved in the conflict to the Sinai to separate Israeli and Egyptian forces and to monitor the truce.

This neutral presence of UN personnel invited into a postconflict situation by two contending parties is now known as "classical peacekeeping."

With a few exceptions, the peace operations sponsored or approved by the United Nations during the cold war era did not involve troops as combatants. The major exception was the UN-approved use of force by the United States against North Korea. Another important exception was the UN-sponsored peace operation in the Congo, which involved combatants operating under the UN flag. A minor exception was the Security Council's approval in 1966 of an enforcement action by Great Britain against an oil tanker whose cargo was headed for Rhodesia and was therefore violating the UN trade embargo. For the most part, UN peace operations during the cold war period involved conflicts between nations that the UN attempted to freeze or contain, but the UN's missions in Cyprus and Palestine did establish a precedent for UN involvement in civil conflicts.

New Dimensions of Peacekeeping

In the late 1980s and early 1990s there was a tremendous expansion in UN peace operations. However, it was not so much the increased number of operations as the changing character of UN peace interventions that distinguished this period.

Among the new features of post-cold war peace operations have been the declining importance given to considerations of national sovereignty, the increasing importance of humanitarian concerns, the multiplicity of mission objectives, the heightened influence of the United States, and the willingness to put the UN stamp of approval on peace operations carried out separately by member nations. As the Council for a Livable World Education Fund's report pointed out, "Recent operations have challenged traditional grounds for peacekeepers and stretched the definition of peacekeeping and peace operations." [7]

The new dimensions of UN peacekeeping are part of what some critics call the militarization of the United Nations, meaning that the social and developmental work of the world body is being overshadowed by the UN's involvement in or approval of military missions. Secretary General Boutros-Ghali heightened these concerns when he said: "The United States is not eager to play the role of the policeman of the world. So the United Nations is there to do the job."[8] Although multilateral military responses to global conflicts must be part of the UN's mission, the control exercised by the United States sparks valid concerns about UN-approved military interventions decided on and directed solely by the U.S. government.

The idea of the United Nations as an embryonic form of world government has been held by many of the UN's strongest supporters.

Sovereignty Losing Ground

The United Nations is just that—an organization of nations, not of people or their organizations. The founding principle of the United Nations was the collective security of nations, and the concept of national self-determination and sovereignty was the foundation of the new world order that emerged after World War II. No

longer was colonialism considered the acceptable
method for arranging global affairs. Indeed, decolonization became a central focus for the General Assembly.
Peace and justice were seen almost exclusively through
the prisms of sovereignty and self-determination.
International peace and security were at risk when a
nation's sovereignty was violated, and justice was at

Promoting cooperation. Port au Prince, Haiti.

stake when a colonized people's right to self-determination was not honored.

Although the legitimacy of the nation-state has been a
guiding principle of the United Nations, the organization
has since its beginning also harbored universalist goals
that helped undermine the primacy of national boundaries. The idea of the United Nations as an embryonic
form of world government rather than as simply a collection of states has been held by many of the UN's

strongest supporters, particularly those activists and organizations associated with the peace and antinuclear movements. The incorporation within the UN Charter of broad humanitarian goals concerning the welfare of all peoples reflected this universalist sentiment, and the UN-sponsored conventions on human rights and natural resource conservation have also reflected the erosion of the primacy of the nation-state. Indicative of the ascendancy of universalism was the arms embargo against South Africa, begun in 1963, and the suspension of its UN membership in 1974 because of its domestic policies of apartheid.

During the UN's first fifty years, there was an expanding international awareness that the condition of individual basic rights could not be overlooked when considering international peace and security issues. Often, however, the importance of protecting human rights came into conflict with the notion of the inviolability of national sovereignty. Similarly, the increasing awareness of earth as the common home for the world's population placed ecology in conflict with statehood. At the same time that such theoretical and moral considerations were eroding the concept of national sovereignty, technological innovations and global economic integration also whittled away at the notion of a world defined by separate and independent nations. In 1991, expressing the evolving limits of sovereignty, former Secretary General Javier Pérez de Cuéllar said, "We are clearly witnessing what is an irresistible shift in public attitudes towards the belief that defense of the oppressed in the name of morality should prevail over frontiers and legal documents." [9]

This gradual erosion of the hallowed principle of national sovereignty has met with some resistance.

Many of the less developed nations have been the firmest defenders of the principle. Fearing a return to the colonial order in which the world's most powerful nations determine what is right, they have voted in the United Nations against any measure that could be regarded as infringing on the sovereignty of another nation. Declarations of universal standards of human rights have also met the objections of countries like Singapore and China, who claim that the Western world is trying to impose its own standards on less privileged states.[10] Similarly, some industrialized nations, notably the United States, have vigorously opposed measures that would broaden the concept of human rights to include economic rights and might thereby threaten the free flow of goods and capital.

The conflicting notions of national sovereignty were very much evident in the 1988-95 period.[11] The most dramatic decision of the Security Council came in defense of national sovereignty when it approved the United States to lead a non-UN multilateral force to repel the Iraqi invasion of Kuwait. With respect to UN-sponsored peace operations, most involved UN forces in what would have been previously regarded as the purely domestic affairs of member nations. In most cases, the United Nations was invited into the country to resolve an internal conflict, such as in El Salvador, but in the cases of Bosnia and Somalia the United Nations undertook peace operations without the consent of all the conflicting forces.

In the name of such values as democracy, humanitarian assistance, and the protection of persecuted minorities, the United Nations has directed or approved of peace missions throughout the world. In the flush of new international attention given to UN peace operations, UN

Secretary General Boutros Boutros-Ghali declared that "the centuries-old doctrine of absolute and exclusive sovereignty no longer stands."

The new willingness of the Security Council to violate national sovereignty in the name of universal principles became evident when it forced Iraq to accept UN intervention to assist and protect its Kurdish population. No such measures were considered for Turkey or Iran, both of which have large repressed Kurdish populations. In adopting a resolution that defined Iraq's repression of its own civilians as a threat "to international peace and security in the region," the United Nations further battered down the protections offered in international law to sovereign states and increased the potential for UN interventionism.

The experience in Somalia led to generalized disillusion about the capabilities of the United Nations.

The UN-sanctioned intervention by the United States in Somalia highlighted the new post-cold war interventionism. The stated objective was not so much to bring peace and stability to this anarchic land but to provide humanitarian assistance to its population. The intervention in Somalia, while clearly signaling a more ambitious and interventionist sentiment in the Security Council, had a political backdrop. Although the reasons for the humanitarian disaster and climate of violence were multiple, the long and sordid history of being alternately supplied with arms by the United States and the Soviet Union during the cold war was probably the primary cause for the chaotic conditions in Somalia. While there was no doubt that Somalians badly needed humanitarian assistance, the UN-authorized operation by the United States in Somalia raised questions as to why there were not similar interventions in places such as East Timor, Sudan, Western Sahara, Mozambique, and Liberia.

In the end, the humanitarian intervention in Somalia did not turn out as well as its supporters had hoped. Instead, it proved to be a quagmire in which UN-sponsored troops operated not as neutral peacekeeping forces but as a party to the fighting. The experience in Somalia, rather than bestowing greater confidence in the new world order heralded by President Bush, led to generalized disillusion about the capabilities of the United Nations. The UN's mission in the former Yugoslavia heightened this sense of disillusion and deception about UN peace operations.

In both cases, the actual humanitarian assistance was largely successful in terms of caring for people and saving lives. The problem was that these missions did little or nothing to achieve peace and security, and the Somalia and Bosnia missions also raised questions about whether the United Nations had the capability and resources for these humanitarian interventions. Largely overlooked in the escalating criticism of the United Nations was the way the United States and the western European nations scapegoated the United Nations as a way to cover the failures of their own foreign policies.

At the same time that the world was witnessing frightening outbreaks of ethnic violence, signs of failing governmental structures, new secession battles, and fundamentalist and other extremist challenges to state power, the United Nations was faced with a financial crisis and the unwillingness of member nations to increase their commitment to a permanent peacekeeping capability within the UN structure. The UN's financial crisis reflected the declining political will of members nations, particularly the United States, to commit national troops in foreign conflicts that had no direct relationship to their own security. Failures in Somalia and Bosnia, together with signs that earlier successes in places such as Cambodia were breaking down, contributed to what some have called "compassion fatigue." This term refers to a rising concern that alongside the new world order of economic globalization and the absence of bipolar tensions is a new world disorder whose problems are too complex and pervasive for the resources and remedies at hand. It is a perception of international affairs that has been strengthened by the worsening social and economic problems facing the world's wealthier nations and by a deepening conviction that the national interests of the United States and other global powers should be more narrowly defined.

Multidimensioned Operations

The move away from classical peacekeeping to humanitarian assistance and other interventions within what were or had been sovereign nations made UN peace operations more difficult to categorize. Within the same peacekeeping mission, there could commonly be found a wide range of UN activities. At the same time that the United Nations was called upon to supervise and monitor elections, as part of its peace operations it also became involved in land reform, monitoring human rights, directing reconstruction, disarming combatants, launching military attacks, protecting noncombatants, delivering humanitarian assistance and protecting food convoys, and assisting refugees and internally displaced people. In the former Yugoslavia, at the same time that UN peacekeeping forces were trying to maintain a neutral stance, the Security Council authorized NATO bombing missions. In Somalia, a humanitarian mission was paralleled by search-and-destroy missions led by U.S. troops.

As the dimensions of peacekeeping expanded, the United Nations was also being called upon to perform (and was assuming) the role of nationbuilding. When societies and governments disintegrated, thereby threatening regional peace and security, the United Nations was the institution expected to reorder and stabilize nations. At the same time that the parameters of UN peacekeeping expanded, other UN concerns, such as the condition of human rights and the plight of refugees, were not adequately addressed.

By 1995 the UN secretary-general had backed away from his earlier statements about the capability and willingness of the United Nations to involve itself in situations that went beyond classical peacekeeping. This backpedalling reflected the declining support for the United Nations in Washington, where President Clinton had dropped earlier commitments to multilateralism and UN peacekeeping as central to his foreign policy. Secretary General Boutros-Ghali recognized that the ambitious vision that he had laid out in his *Agenda for Peace* was not possible without the strong backing of the United States. This rising reluctance on the part of both the UN Secretariat and the member nations to support new peacekeeping operations was made all too evident by the failure of the Security Council, mainly due to the lack of U.S. approval, to take action to stop the genocide in Rwanda in 1994.

UN Surrogates

The Security Council's authorization of the U.S. military response to the Iraqi takeover of Kuwait was not unprecedented. The Gulf War had its antecedent in the Korean War, in which the United Nations counted on U.S. troops to repel the North Koreans. Recognizing its inability to mobilize the forces to act decisively, the United Nations has shown increased willingness to allow regional powers to undertake missions on its behalf. This was the case with the United States in the Persian Gulf (1990-91) and in Haiti together with the Organization of American States (1994); with NATO in the former Yugoslavia (1992-present); and with the controversial and largely ineffective action by France in Rwanda (1994). In addition, the United Nations

With the cold war over, intervening nations and institutions now seek the UN mantle of approval for their actions.

has stood on the sidelines or signaled its approval (as in Georgia and Tajikistan) as Russia has attempted to exercise its military influence in what that country calls its "near abroad."

This approval of peace operations by regional hegemons, former colonial powers, and regional alliances can be seen as a delegation of authority by the United Nations and a recognition of the limitations of the UN's peacekeeping capabilities. With the cold war over and colonialism no longer an acceptable manner of managing international relations, intervening nations and institutions now seek the UN mantle of approval for their actions. But when UN sponsorship appears unlikely, as in the case of the U.S. invasion of Panama (1989), a regional power can act alone and suffer only a temporary setback in its international public stature.

Regional alliances, such as those of NATO and the OAS, offer a better alternative than actions undertaken by individual nations. In the Middle East and Asia, no regional organization can claim widespread support. In Africa, the Organization of African Unity (OAU) lacks the resources and training to undertake successful peace missions. There also exists the problem that single states dominate some regional organizations, examples being Nigeria in the Economic Community of West African States (ECOWAS) and the United States in the OAS.

As Chapter VIII of the UN Charter asserts, a rising role for regional and subregional groups in international affairs is consistent with the goals of the United Nations. Although there are advantages to having regional organizations involved in settling area conflicts, there is a danger that these organizations may operate less in the interests of the conflictive country and more in the interests of the dominant nations within the regional group. The involvement of the OAS in the U.S. occupation of the Dominican Republic in 1965 and the Warsaw Pact's endorsement of the Soviet Union's occupation of Czechoslovakia in 1968 are reminders of the dubious credibility of some regional organizations. Alternatively, recent OAS resolutions regarding Haiti, Guatemala, and El Salvador highlight the effective role that regional organizations can play in facilitating peace.

Managing and Budgeting

The founding nations of the United Nations assumed that member states would designate armed forces and facilities to allow the creation of a standing UN military. Cold war tensions and concerns about national sovereignty kept this internationalist vision from becoming a reality. In the wake of the cold war and with increasing calls for UN peacekeeping forces around the world, there are still many advocates for peacekeeping forces that would be on-call and could be rapidly deployed to areas of incipient conflict. Related proposals call for an increase in UN intelligence gathering and logistics capacities, a financing system that would not depend on ad hoc contributions, the designation of particular units of national armies as international peacekeeping forces, and the joint training of these units from different nations.

It is certainly true that the present system of financing and deployment of peacekeeping forces is less than satisfactory. Because there is no standing UN army or on-call troops, each peace operation requires its own budget, equipment requisition plan, and troop call-up. This means that troops from the various nations that have agreed to supply solders often arrive late at the operation area and come poorly equipped and untrained for the mission.[12] Short of creating a UN army, the establishment of stockpiles of commonly used peacekeeping equipment located throughout the world is one frequent recommendation for improving UN peacekeeping efficiency and response time.

Since peacekeeping is not a centralized function, each peace operation depends on ad hoc assessment of member states. UN peacekeeping missions are funded largely through special assessments and to a much smaller degree from regular budget assessments and voluntary contributions.[13] Depending on their size and economic conditions, all countries are assessed at a percentage of their regular UN budget assessments. Security Council members have agreed—in recognition of their special responsibility in matters of international peace and security—to contribute at least 20 percent more than their regular assessments.[14]

Even more than the UN's general budget, the peace operations budget is in a constant state of financial uncertainty. One reason is the rapid increase in the cost of peacekeeping operations, rising from $183 million in 1986 to $3.3 billion in 1995. Nearly 60 percent of the $16 billion in cumulative peacekeeping expenses in the UN's fifty year history came in the 1992-95 period. Most nations do not pay their peace operations assessments on time; 85 percent were late in 1994.[15] At the end of 1995 the UN's top contributors owed about $2 billion in assessments for peacekeeping—up from $363 million in 1987 and nearly double the $1.2 billion in arrears registered at the end of 1994.[16] Peacekeeping arrears inhibit the United Nations from undertaking new peace operations, as critical as they may be.

In 1992 the General Assembly created a Peacekeeping Reserve Fund of $150 million to finance the start-up costs of new missions. But because of mounting peacekeeping arrears and the need to borrow from the fund to cover ongoing UN operations, the reserve is nonfunctional. Commonly, less than one percent of the reserve is available for new missions. Critics often charge that the United Nations is a mammoth bureaucracy that pays little attention to budget limitations. Although there is certainly much room for improvement in fiscal management, UN peace operations illustrate how difficult it is for the United Nations both to fulfill its global responsibilities and to stay financially solvent.

Idealism and Realism

From its beginnings, the United Nations—its character and possibilities—has been regarded differently by various political camps. In the United States, generally it has been those on the left that have been most supportive of the United Nations, while the right has taken a more critical and cautious stance. Although this categorization is still largely true, there have developed deep fissures in both camps that have much to do with differences as to the proper role for UN peacekeepers.

The U.S.-initiated interventions in Somalia and Haiti were considered to be appropriate and morally justifiable uses of U.S. power.

Throughout much of its history, the United Nations has unfortunately been a stage for ideological battle. The right was united in its criticism of the General Assembly and the UN's development agencies as being instruments to criticize the United States and carry out the left's agenda of class warfare and worldwide revolution. But this criticism from the right did not mean that the left was a strong supporter of the United Nations. The left did, however, value the United Nations as a generally positive force for peace and development.

The end of the cold war and the flurry of UN peace operations since 1988 have reopened the debate about the future of the United Nations and its role in achieving international peace and security. Perhaps the most striking change has been the degree to which leftists and liberals in the United States have lent their support to military intervention in the internal affairs of other nations. In the 1970s when George McGovern proposed UN intervention in Cambodia to stop Pol Pot and the Khmer Rouge, he found little support to the left of center. Many of those who supported his anti-interventionist position in Vietnam were horrified at the suggestion that the United States lend its support to a humanitarian assistance intervention in Cambodia. By the 1990s, however, there was only a smattering of opposition on the left to the UN-approved interventions in Somalia, Haiti, and the former Yugoslavia. It was mostly on the right that one heard strong voices of principled opposition to U.S. involvement in military operations abroad.

The end of the cold war resulted in a resurgence of liberal internationalism in the United States. Whereas U.S. foreign interventions during the cold war were condemned as extensions of U.S. imperialism, the U.S.-initiated interventions in Somalia and Haiti were considered to be appropriate and morally justifiable uses of U.S. power. Wilsonian liberal internationalism had found a new core of support.

Along with the disintegration of the Soviet bloc and the disarray in left-of-center political circles, there also emerged in the late 1980s a new appreciation of the extent and limits of U.S. hegemony. While economic competition made the United States less than the superpower it once was, it was still the world's military and ideological leader. Although the General Assembly still frequently voted against U.S. positions, the United States remained in control of the Security Council and all UN peace operations depended on U.S. cooperation. In most international affairs, but particularly concerning matters of international peace and security, no other nation commanded the hegemonic position maintained by the

United States. There was criticism and carping, yes, but rarely a direct challenge.

The future debate, at least in the United States, about the peacekeeping role of the United Nations is breaking down not according to left-right categories but rather into idealist-realist and internationalist-isolationist tendencies. While the right has long had a strong realist element, it has only been since the end of the cold war that the left has been forced to judge U.S. foreign policy in idealist-realist terms. Leftists have had to ask the hard questions about how—not whether—the United States should exercise its power in world affairs. As the global leader, should the United States now push the United Nations to intervene more to uphold the values of peace, democracy, and multiethnic societies? Or should all UN actions be evaluated solely in terms of their direct benefit to the United States?

Within the Clinton administration, this debate was evidenced in the reversal of an earlier multilateralist position in favor of a position more grounded in what were perceived to be direct U.S. military, political, and economic interests. Idealistic rhetoric gave way to a *realpolitik* more in line with the foreign policies of Nixon and Kissinger. The decision to stand by in the face of the genocidal politics in Rwanda stemmed from this *realpolitik* approach. This does not mean, however, that the United States has retreated into isolationism. If U.S. interests are directly or indirectly involved, as in Haiti and the former Yugoslavia, the United States has demonstrated its willingness to deploy military forces when they are under direct U.S. control.

Global idealism and liberal internationalism should be tempered not only by an assessment of U.S. capacity and interests but also by a recognition of the dangers of interventionism. Only rarely is intervention good for the intervened, and generally the interests of the intervening force, not those of the intervened, are what is really at stake.

At the United Nations, the idealism and internationalist interventionism that characterized the immediate post-cold war period soon gave way to a more hard-nosed assessment of peace operations. On the heels of Clinton's PDD-25 in May 1994, the United Nations adopted a similar stance guiding future involvement in peacekeeping. Within a few weeks the Security Council outlined factors for the conduct and evaluation of UN peace operations, including the following:

- whether international peace and security is threatened;
- availability of other means or organizations, such as regional groups like NATO or the OAS, to help resolve the crisis;
- existence of a cease-fire and an invitation to the United Nations to intervene with the consent of the involved parties;
- clear political goal and precise mandate for the operation; and
- ensured security of UN personnel.

A UN resolution establishing a peace operation is expected to lay out the mandate (citing the provision of the UN Charter), the proposed date of the mission's expiration, and the date for the review period to begin. In addition, the UN Secretariat must identify expected funding sources and estimate the expected costs of the peace operation.

The initial post-cold war enthusiasm for using the United Nations to keep or make peace has faded. Caution about launching new UN peacekeeping efforts represents a healthy response to the failure of the United Nations to define the goals, limits, and dimensions of maintaining international peace and security. Unfortunately, the failures, inadequacies, and successes of recent peace missions have not spurred the United States and other UN members to commit themselves to a more cohesive vision of collective security and peace-keeping. Instead, the nations of the world tend to react too late to threats to global peace and to rely too heavily on traditional policies of national security.

Chapter Five

Selected Peace Operations: Lessons to Learn

This chapter takes a brief look at several UN peace operations in order to illustrate the kinds of problems encountered during these missions and to point the way to reforms that could make UN peacekeeping more effective.

Angola

The persistence of political violence in Angola and the failures of the United Nations can be largely attributed to foreign involvement. By supporting the UNITA terrorist counterrevolutionaries led by Jonas Savimbi, the United States in the 1980s propagated an internal conflict as part of its international campaign against all leftist governments. In 1989 a UN peace mission successfully monitored the withdrawal of Cuban troops who had been aiding the Angolan government. The UN mission then helped arrange a cease-fire and elections in 1992 as part of a peace accord brokered by Portugal. However, a lack of interest by the major world powers allowed the construction of a weak peace accord in which implementation was left to the warring factions with no provision for political powersharing. The results of the elections, regarded as free and fair by the United Nations and other observers, were rejected by the UNITA rebels, who had been soundly defeated, and civil war resumed. Another cease-fire was arranged by the United Nations in May 1995, and an agreement was reached in which, in return for ending the war, UNITA's Savimbi became Angola's vice-president. More than 200,000 lives were lost in the 1992-95 period. Although the civil war has at least temporarily ended, the UN peace mission cannot be regarded as a success. The mission was undermined by the lack of strong UN commitment, by pro-UNITA sympathies and support on the part of the United States, and by the precipitous manner in which elections were embraced as a quick solution. The United Nations failed to provide a peacekeeping force large enough to monitor the cease-fire and demobilize the rebels, and it failed to ensure that the results of the elections would be respected by the losing party. The dominance of the United States in UN affairs prevented the United Nations from acting early on to meet the threat to regional peace posed by the UNITA contras in the 1980s. The UN's peace mission in Angola is an example of the inevitable problems of peacekeeping carried out on the cheap and without the muscle of the major powers.

To be successful, UN peace operations need the sustained attention of the United Nations and its firm financial support. The Angola operation suffered as world attention switched to Somalia, the former Yugoslavia, Cambodia, and the former Soviet Union. As a result, the United Nations, whose resources were being drained, left the implementation of the peace accord to the belligerent parties—a certain recipe for failure. If the international community is serious about helping to resolve internal conflicts in a peaceful manner, it must give the United Nations the financing and peacekeeping infrastructure such an effort deserves.

Cambodia

The peace operation in Cambodia was a product of post-cold war enthusiasm for resolving civil conflicts. Because members of the Security Council were involved, the United Nations stood passively by during the U.S. bombing of the country after the U.S.-sponsored coup in 1970 and during the genocidal campaign (at least one million killed) by the Khmer Rouge following its takeover of the state in 1975. Nor did the United Nations act to prevent the Vietnamese from installing a new Cambodian government in 1979 as part their invasion of Cambodia in response to continued provocations by the Khmer Rouge. Although the Vietnamese-installed government lacked legitimacy, it did succeed in restoring order to much of the country since both the Vietnamese and the Cambodian army severely weakened the Khmer Rouge.

In its effort to remain neutral, the United Nations failed to recognize that the continued existence of the Khmer Rouge was the main threat to the peace process.

The Vietnamese-supported Hun Sen government was opposed by several armed groups, including the Khmer Rouge, who initially joined together in support of the UN mission to effect a democratic transition. The UN mission did succeed in securing the withdrawal of

Killing Fields Memorial. Phnom Penh, Cambodia

Vietnamese troops, facilitating free elections, and installing a new coalition government. Engaging 15,000 troops and 7,000 civilians at a cost of $2.8 billion, UNTAC represents the largest UN peace operation to date. This multifunctional operation—demobilization, refugee resettlement, election monitoring, and support for the formation of a civilian government—established the important precedent of involving most of the population in democratic elections. But UNTAC failed to bring peace to Cambodia. Without a peace enforcement mandate, UNTAC lacked the capacity to demobilize the Khmer Rouge, which attempted to undermine both the election and the transition process.

The overriding concern of the UN mission was to ensure the removal of Vietnamese troops and to end Vietnamese control of the government. By those standards the mission was successful. Neither China, which had long supported the Khmer Rouge, nor the United States wanted to allow Vietnam to develop into a regional power in Southeast Asia. The Soviet Union, Vietnam's traditional supporter on the Security Council, had collapsed, while its successor, the Russian Federation, was eager to gain favor with the Western powers.

As in Angola, elections in Cambodia were held before the United Nations was able to guarantee a cease-fire and the demobilization of antigovernment armies. Too much emphasis was placed on holding free elections and removing the Vietnam-backed government, while not enough was done to ensure peace and stability.

The May 1993 election was the first that the United Nations directly organized from the planning stage through the drafting of the electoral law to the administration of the voting. But in its effort to remain neutral, the United Nations failed to recognize that the continued existence of the Khmer Rouge was the main threat to the peace process. It failed to demobilize this outlaw army and failed to enforce the anti-Khmer Rouge embargo, in part due to the heterogeneous nature of the peacekeeping mission. In Cambodia, the United Nations fell far short of its nationbuilding objectives, and—in the absence of a strong resolve on the part of the Security Council to stand up to Pol Pot—failed in its main mission to protect Cambodians from the scourge of war and the continuing threats of the Khmer Rouge. Rather than enhancing the UN's reputation, UNTAC tarnished its credibility. The experience in Cambodia points to the need for more realistic and better coordinated UN peacekeeping operations. If the United Nations becomes involved in conflictive situations, it must be given the authority and capability to force belligerents to comply with negotiated peace accords. As it is, peace enforcement occurs only when major powers commit themselves militarily.

El Salvador

The UN mission in El Salvador successfully brokered an end to the 12-year war through peace accords that resulted in the demobilization of the FMLN guerrillas, the downsizing of the military, the creation of a new national police force, the monitoring of human rights, and the holding of elections in which the left participated for the first time. This UN effort was a model for multidimensional peace missions that go beyond simply monitoring cease-fires to addressing some of the underlying causes of the conflict. The presence of UN observers in the country during the pre-election period helped ensure the implementation of the peace accords, although both the military and the government were negligent in meeting all their obligations. The success of the UN mission depended on the support of the United States, which had previously been a chief party in the conflict. The deteriorating social and economic conditions for the poor majority in El Salvador, while not directly the responsibility of the United Nations, indicate the need for better coordination among international institutions responsible for social and economic development.

Haiti

The UN involvement in Haiti was another case of intervention in the internal affairs of a nation. But unlike in Somalia, El Salvador, and many other UN peace missions, the mission in Haiti did not concern the resolution of civil strife. Instead, the issue was the toppling of a democratically elected government by a military coup and the associated violations of human rights. Although the Security Council gave its stamp of approval on the U.S. occupation and authorized a UN peace mission that followed on the heels of the U.S. intervention, the United Nations was not a key player in the Haiti crisis. During the crisis revolving around the military coup led by Lieutenant-General Ráoul Cédras and the subsequent efforts to restore Jean-Bertrand Aristide to the presidency, Haiti was regarded as within the sphere of influence of the United States, just as it was under the dictatorships of François and Jean-Claude Duvalier.

Despite the UN's formal involvement in the attempt to restore democratic governance in Haiti, it was the United States that called the shots, even to the extent of not informing the United Nations of its negotiating strategy and military plans. This marginalization of the United Nations resulted in the resignation of the UN emissary to Haiti. The U.S. occupation and the UN peace mission, which was controlled by the U.S. military, did succeed in restoring democracy to Haiti. To the credit of the Clinton administration, the intervention was restrained and, unlike other direct interventions in Grenada and Panama, did gain the support of both the United Nations and the OAS.

But the essentially unilateral intervention points to the continuing problem of having an international entity responsible for global peace and welfare that primarily responds to the concerns of the major powers. In the case of Haiti, the U.S. interest in removing the military government stemmed primarily from its anxiety about the increasing flow of refugees. If the United Nations only authorized peacekeeping operations within the spheres of influence of the major powers, many countries and peoples would be left defenseless.

The Haiti case reaffirms the need for a better policy on sanctions, a more proactive crisis-prevention commitment, and a more constrained policy of relying on regional powers like the United States to carry out UN work. The United States, which had uncritically supplied and trained Haiti's repressive military, has been more interested in political stability in this nearby Caribbean nation than in respect for human rights, social justice, and democratic governance. This concern for stability explains why the U.S. government did not act more quickly to protect the fragile democracy of the leftwing populist Aristide, who was regarded as a threat to the traditional social order in Haiti and, by extension, to other Caribbean societies. Given the long history of U.S.-supported military rule and the Haitian elite's enmity toward Aristide, the United Nations should have taken measures to discourage a likely military coup and exercised more control over the U.S. government's peacekeeping intervention.

The UN-authorized trade sanctions against Haiti were weak and not enforced. Finally, when the sanctions were tightened, they were not given sufficient time to work. In the end, Washington decided, mostly due to the escalating refugee crisis, that its interests in stability and stopping the flow of refugees to U.S. shores would be better served by reinstalling the popular Aristide than in allowing the former CIA and military collaborators to maintain control. Like in El Salvador, the democratization process in Haiti was given new life. But unless the United Nations and other international institutions commit themselves to shaping and supporting policies that promote broad economic development, the prospects for social and economic stability in Haiti are not good.

Somalia

The operation in Somalia was a case study in how not to conduct a peacekeeping effort. Before the United Nations could resolve the crisis caused by Somalia's complex system of clan identity and fueled by cold war meddling, the United States moved in to take its place as peacekeeper. As the U.S. initiative faltered, so too did domestic public opinion, spurring Washington to return the baton to the United Nations officially while still maintaining operational control. The United Nations then became a convenient scapegoat for failed U.S. policies.

The current crisis began in 1991 when military dictator Siad Barre was overthrown. After Barre was disposed a power vacuum developed, leading to an outbreak of clan conflicts and a disintegration of the Somali state. During the cold war, Barre had been supported alternately by Washington and Moscow with generous economic and military aid packages. With access to the modern weapons formerly controlled by the police state, rivalries between clans, led by Ali Mahdi and Mohammad Farah Aidid, degenerated into widespread massacres and looting. The hostilities resulted in widespread death and destruction, forcing hundreds of thousands of civilians to flee their homes and creating a dire need for emergency humanitarian assistance. Almost 4.5 million people in Somalia—over half of the estimated population—were threatened by severe malnutrition and malnutrition-related disease, with the most affected living in the countryside. A drought aggravated the situation, and the International Red Cross declared that famine and political chaos had created an international emergency—one in which a estimated 500,000 people had died in a two-year period. In 1992 the Security Council authorized the first peace mission mandated solely to enforce humanitarian objectives. Ambassador Sakhnoun, the UN Special Representative for the mission, never received Security Council support for his daring peace plan that involved working with—rather than against—the clans to reestablish order. Opposition, mainly by the United States, led to his resignation before his plan could be implemented. Given the abundance of arms, the lack of credible political leadership, and the extent of misery, it was by no means certain that Sakhnoun's plan would have actually worked.

The Security Council members, particularly the United States, resisted giving the UN peace mission the strength it needed. When the Security Council finally authorized 3,000 troops for the operation in addition to the fifty observers placed in the country in April 1992, most countries other than Pakistan declined to provide volunteers, rendering the mission little more than a simple token of UN goodwill. Diplomatic efforts of the OAU and the League of Arab States were also ineffective in consolidating the cease-fire brokered by the United Nations on March 3, 1992.

The failure of the UN mission to secure the cease-fire or to effectively support famine relief led to the approval of a unilateral "humanitarian intervention" by the United States involving 30,000 troops. The Security Council in December 1992 authorized the United States to "use all necessary means to establish as soon as possible a secure environment for humanitarian relief operations." Occurring during the final month of the Bush administration, the U.S. venture was widely regarded as an attempt to bolster the reputation of the outgoing president. Although humanitarian concerns certainly played a part in the decision to intervene, the Somalia operation could also be seen as a way for Washington to assert international leadership without having to involve U.S. troops in the apparently more risky conflict in Bosnia.

Under the U.S. command, UN peacekeeping and humanitarian intervention soon boiled down to a peace enforcement mission in which U.S. troops focused on hunting down the warlord Aidid.

The initial humanitarian mission was overshadowed and distorted by a military mission defined by the United States.

The initial mission—to provide and protect humanitarian assistance—was overshadowed and distorted by a military mission defined by the United States. The mission arrived in Mogadishu with a limited and unclear mandate, leading to a weak, uncoordinated response. The U.S. attempt to organize local police forces was half-hearted and, when combined with selective searches for weapons, raised questions about the neutrality of the mission. These problems, coupled with rising domestic concern, prompted Washington to return the mission to the United Nations. In May 1993 the United Nations took over the U.S. mission, authorizing its second peace mission in Somalia. The United States continued to play a role in the UN mission, having secured the appointment of a retired U.S. admiral to direct the operation. The UN mission also retained U.S. military objectives rather than limiting itself to humanitarian aid, thereby continuing the errors of the U.S.-directed mission.

The second UN mission was doomed after a raid on General Aidid's headquarters on October 3, 1993 backfired. Seventeen U.S. troops died, and 78 were wounded. The Clinton administration, in an attempt to deflect criticism, blamed the United Nations for the soldiers' deaths even though the raid was carried out without the knowledge of other UN troops and was directly under a U.S. command.

The failures and shortcomings of the Somalia peace operations included: not disarming all the warlords simultaneously; mixing humanitarian and military missions; allowing some national peacekeeping troops to operate independently, thereby creating rivalries and discord among the various UN peacekeeping forces; and turning over the mission to a single nation (United States) whose motives and commitment to the Somali people were questionable. UN authorities deserve blame for not developing a cohesive humanitarian assistance and peacekeeping strategy for Somalia. In the end, however, the responsibility for the tragedy of the Somalia case rests with Security Council members for their failure to support strong peacekeeping and diplomatic efforts at the first signs of the crisis, and for militarizing a humanitarian assistance operation without providing clear political or military objectives. Yet the U.S. and UN missions, despite all their failings, did succeed in saving many Somali lives by ensuring the delivery of humanitarian aid.

Former Yugoslavia

The breakup of Yugoslavia and the subsequent outbreak of nationalist and interethnic warfare highlight the new challenges of defining and maintaining collective security in the post-cold war era. In the Balkan strife, the major Western powers, namely the United States, Britain, Germany, and France, relegated the United Nations to a minor, albeit important, role, namely providing humanitarian assistance to the besieged Bosnians. While the Western powers bickered over what to do about the crisis, they conveniently avoided taking more decisive action by foisting most of the public blame for the continuing atrocities onto the United Nations. Unlike in Somalia, where the "humanitarian intervention" did not maintain the pretense of neutrality but instead singled out certain warlords for capture or elimination, the UN mission in Bosnia was instructed to maintain strict neutrality, even when the distinction between victims and perpetrators was easily made. By creating the illusion that something was being done to stop the atrocities, the UN presence in Bosnia may have actually prolonged the war. It was left to the United States and the NATO powers to broker a peace accord in 1995 that led to a cease-fire and a plan that implicitly accepted territorial division along ethnic lines established during the war.

The case of the former Yugoslavia is further evidence of the need for an active diplomatic capacity in the Secretariat that would use the good offices of the United Nations to negotiate solutions to imminent conflicts. The United Nations, with the support of its most influential and affected members, should have, for example, immediately formulated a unified plan to support leaders within the former Yugoslav Federation who sought to prevent Croatia and Slovenia from seceding. As it was, differences between the EC nations, Russia, and the United States created the opening in which the conflicts among the former Yugoslav states intensified.

Clearly, there should have been an international effort to maintain the multiethnic confederation of Yugoslavia rather than acceding to nationalist campaigns that soon devolved into wars of ethnic cleansing. The crisis in the former Yugoslavia also points to the need for a better policy on sanctions and their enforcement, given how ineffective the sanctions were in the case of the Serbs. In addition, the Balkan quagmire also underlines the need for a more developed peacekeeping policy that would keep UN Blue Helmets from becoming defenseless victims. The UN's peacekeeping missions reflect its inability to muster the necessary forces or political will needed to successfully conclude operations.

The peace settlement signed in Dayton, Ohio, in December 1995 maintained the illusion of reestablishing a multiethnic confederation, but in effect it sanctioned the ethnic divisions created by the warring factions. The settlement made no direct provisions for prosecuting those accused of gross violations of human rights, although it did bind the signatories to cooperate with the war crimes tribunal in The Hague.

Keeping the United Nations weak and dependent on the interests of the Western powers led to the unattractive option of an intervention by NATO powers operating with little moral authority. The United Nations should be credited, however, for its mission in Macedonia, which serves as a model of how a small UN peacekeeping force, serving as a kind of trip wire, can help prevent a conflict from escalating into a regional war.

The situation in the former Yugoslavia illustrates the difficulty of establishing a new world order that seeks to maintain peace and to halt gross abuses of human rights in places where political leaders demonstrate little will to negotiate an end to the conflict and where borders separating the conflicting forces are not well-defined. Though the UN response was certainly inadequate, the mobilization of a peace enforcement contingent was clearly beyond the capacity of the United Nations. The world body must either improve its peacekeeping capabilities or the world will have to continue to hope that the interests of organizations like NATO and military powers like the United States coincide with the UN's mission to maintain world peace. It should be recognized, however, that military intervention—either by the United Nations or by regional powers—is not always appropriate. The United Nations should pursue all nonmilitary means to prevent or end conflicts, and military action should be taken or approved in internal disputes only when there is good reason to believe that a successful resolution is likely. In any event, in the case of such a grave violation of international peace, the United Nations should not be sidelined as it was in the former Yugoslavia but should be the principal forum for peacekeeping strategy and, ideally, the primary international channel for peacekeeping operations.

Chapter Six

Global Economy and Society

It is commonly recognized that the forces of globalization—free flow of capital, rise of transnational corporations, integrated marketing and production, and
technological and communications advances—are
diminishing the power of states to determine their own
economic development policies. At the same time that
control of nation-states has decreased, the power and
influence of transnational corporations (TNCs) and multilateral financial institutions have greatly expanded in
the past fifty years. Of the world's one-hundred largest
economic units, more than forty are industrial corporations. Many of the world's financial companies and retail
corporations also have more economic impact than individual nations (Appendix 1).

This globalization has not occurred in isolation from
the international organizations that were created in the
aftermath of World War II. In fact, such institutions as
the World Bank, the IMF, and GATT/World Trade
Organization have fostered this globalization through
their own policies, economic modernization projects,
lending programs, and ideological stances.

The United Nations has also played a role in globalization. By working to maintain international peace and security, the world body has helped create a more stable global climate for trade and investment. Through its developmental, environmental, and social programs, the United Nations has also helped mitigate the impact of unregulated capitalism, thereby allowing the multilateral banks and trading organizations to focus on improving the economic structures for development. By establishing common global standards in such areas as air transportation, weather reporting, and mail delivery, the United Nations and its associated agencies have also facilitated economic globalization.

Yet the need for better coordination between global economic, social, and environmental policies is becoming increasingly urgent. To some degree, the environmental and labor side agreements of the North American Free Trade Agreement (NAFTA) illustrated this new consciousness. But as NAFTA critics charged, those agreements did not reflect the need for fundamental integration of social, environmental, and economic considerations.

In the global arena, the United Nations is clearly the most appropriate organization to guide international development. Language in the UN Charter gives it this responsibility and authority. It empowers the General Assembly to "promote international cooperation in the economic, social, cultural, educational, and health fields." Another section of the Charter reads: "With a view to the creation of conditions of stability and well-being which are necessary for peaceful and friendly relations among nations based on respect for the principle of equal rights and self-determination of peoples, the United Nations shall promote higher standards of living;

full employment and conditions of economic and social progress and development; solutions of international economic, social, health, and related problems; and international cultural and educational cooperation."

The United Nations has not shirked this responsibility. Indeed, many of its agencies have been at the forefront of the social and economic advancement of the global population. Such agencies as the UN Conference on Trade and Development (UNCTAD) and the UN Industrial Development Organization (UNIDO), established in the 1960s, have furthered efforts by the less developed nations to address the inequities in the international economic system. In the course of their work these international bodies have endured regular attacks by the world's more developed nations together with corporations and rightwing ideologues. Before undergoing restructuring and downsizing in recent years, these agencies regularly published reports and hosted forums that argued that the differences between the wealthy and poor nations must be addressed by altering inequitable patterns of trade and investment.[1]

The United Nations has helped mitigate the impact of unregulated capitalism.

Alert to the rise of transnational corporations, the United Nations created a center to study TNCs and to help nations regulate them. Concerned about deepening polarization between industrialized nations and less developed ones, many members in the early 1970s called for the creation of a New International Economic Order (NIEO) to help reshape global trading relationships in ways that would gradually narrow the gap between the poorest and wealthiest nations.[2] It would do this by having countries declare a moratorium on their external debt, create a code of conduct for TNCs, increase market openings for third world exports, establish higher prices for raw materials by establishing buffer stocks of commodities, and facilitate technology transfer to less developed countries. Furthermore, advocates of the NIEO asserted that countries should have the right to choose their own economic and political systems without interference by either multilateral financial institutions or foreign powers.

UN attempts to address the structural causes of economic polarization and widening poverty have met with opposition in the United States and other wealthy nations. At the same time that the Bretton Woods institutions have received strong support, the UN's development activities associated with the priorities of less developed nations have been heavily criticized. Among the main institutions targeted by those calling for the downsizing of the United Nations are UNCTAD, ILO, FAO, UNDP, and UNIDO.

A further expression of this antipathy to all measures that might be seen as potentially threatening to market-driven globalization, according to Princeton's professor Richard Falk, a close observer of UN affairs, "has been resistance to the treatment of economic and social rights as deserving of inclusion within the category of human rights by those seeking to confine UN human rights activities to the protection of the individual's civil and political rights. Western opposition to 'the rights of development' reflects the same spirit of resisting any potential claims for redistributive justice in relation to the allocation of resources." [3]

Certainly global economic planning should not take place in isolation from concerns about the environment and social justice. This is, however, exactly what is happening, with the responsibility for the global economic system in the hands of unrepresentative organizations almost exclusively concerned about the health of the market while the fate of society and the environment are addressed by UN agencies and conferences that have little power to affect the flow of international trade and capital.

This lack of an integral approach to globalization is, in large part, an institutional problem. As the world's most representative and open institution and the one with the broadest goals (encompassing social, cultural, economic, educational, environmental, and health issues), the United Nations should be given more authority over matters that are currently the exclusive responsibility of other, more narrowly focused institutions. Yet the disjuncture between economics on the one side and society and the environment on the other cannot be resolved simply with institutional changes. Part of the problem is that the social forces necessary to confront market-driven globalization with a more people- and environment-centered agenda are still weak and disparate.

Fate of the United Nations Center on Transnational Corporations (CTC)

Symptomatic not only of the reduced UN commitment to represent the interests of the world's poor and working people but also of its acceptance of the new global order was the 1993 dismantling of the Center on Transnational Corporations (CTC). The center, which was established in 1974 by the UN Economic and Social

Council, had played a key role in providing information about transnational corporations and in calling for a TNC code of conduct. Founded at a time when the Group of 77 developing countries was demanding that the industrial world join it in creating a new international economic order, the CTC was restructured and downsized at a time when transnational capital had gained a firm hold on global markets and production.[4]

The conversion of the CTC into the Commission on International Investment and Transnational Corporations was part of a 1993 restructuring of many of the UN's economic and social agencies, engineered principally by the United States. Now consolidated as a smaller agency within the weakened UN Conference on Trade and Development, the commission operates with a smaller budget and reduced authority. UNCTAD itself, widely respected for its work on world development issues, is being remodeled, and its position within the UN structure is being downgraded.

Indeed, the transnational commission and UNCTAD have been given a new mission. Instead of attempting to counterbalance the power of TNCs by providing information about their activities and spearheading efforts to regulate them, the new commission has been charged with putting more emphasis on facilitating flows of foreign investment capital and strengthening ties between TNCs and developing countries.[5] Commenting on the revamped role of the commission, Chakravarthi Raghavan (editor of the *South-North Department Monitor*), in a keynote address to a conference of the World Council of Churches, criticized the new agency as complementing the IMF, the World Bank, and the WTO in promoting the interests of TNCs and foreign direct investment.[6]

The United States had no small role in the dissolution of the CTC. In exchange for a promise that the U.S. government would reduce its arrears to the United Nations, Secretary-General Boutros Boutros-Ghali apparently acceded to a Bush administration demand in 1992 to control the appointment of the UN's undersecretary-general of administration and management. Upon his appointment, Richard Thornburgh, the former U.S. attorney general known for his partisanship and rightwing views, secured the shutdown of the CTC.[7]

The CTC had long been an irritant to the United States for its work in drafting a code of conduct for TNCs, including rules requiring disclosure of environmental and occupational hazards of production processes and a ban on the export of goods prohibited as dangerous in their country of origin. It was just when this code of conduct was about to be considered by the representatives to the 1992 Earth Summit in Rio de Janeiro that the CTC was "reorganized." Instead, the summit supported a voluntary code of conduct offered by the Business Council for Sustainable Development, a corporate lobbying group.

Instead of attempting to counterbalance the power of TNCs, the new commission has placed more emphasis on strengthening ties between TNCs and developing countries.

Coordination between the United Nations and the Bretton Woods Institutions

As the globalization of finance, production, communications, and trade deepens, the need for international institutions to guide and regulate the global economy becomes increasingly evident. By virtue of their lending power, the IMF and the World Bank do exert growing influence over international economic matters, particularly in the less developed nations. But these organizations, known as the Bretton Woods Institutions (BWIs), have demonstrated little concern about the impact of their lending programs on social welfare and the environment.

Opposing the global economic order. Kingston, Jamaica.

Critics of these institutions charge that the BWIs represent the narrow economic interests of the world's major economic powers and corporations. Several UN agencies, notably UNICEF and the UNDP, have openly and strongly criticized IMF and World Bank policies for adversely affecting the development prospects of the world's poorer nations. Governments of many nations most severely impacted by these policies have expressed great concern that the role of the United Nations in social and economic affairs has diminished as the UN's emphasis has shifted to security issues.

Both within and outside the United Nations have come proposals to give the world body a new role in coordinating international development programs, including the lending and structural adjustment programs of the BWIs. Advocates of this type of reform assert that the United Nations is a more representative institution and, as such, would help to ensure that development programs do not lead to economic polarization and environmental degradation. In addition, many contend that only by fundamentally changing the relationship between the United Nations and the BWIs can the former become effective as a multilateral institution concerned about global peace, security, and economic welfare.

The UN secretary-general addressed the issue of bringing the United Nations and the BWIs closer together in his 1994 *Agenda for Development*. The *Agenda* stressed the central importance of development and growth with equity and employment generation as well as the need for a new framework for international cooperation. The report also advocated that the United Nations assume a more central role in guiding international economic development.[8]

To pursue these goals, the secretary-general proposed that the UN's Economic and Social Council involve itself in the full range of development issues and that it enter into a "closer relationship" with all the UN's specialized agencies, including the BWIs. Expressing a view common among many international NGOs, Chakravarthi Raghavan suggested that the BWIs: "should be treated as technical institutions in the economic and financial sphere, just as WHO is in the area of health and the ILO in labor issues. But the overall policy thrust and global policy guidance must be set by the UN General Assembly as the main political body of the international community." [9]

The *Agenda for Development* and other proposals calling for a heightened role for the United Nations in international economic matters have not been received favorably by the BWIs. One oft-repeated objection is that BWI policies are based on purely economic considerations and should not be influenced by political pressures, such as those that would come from the United Nations. Responding to proposals for a new role for ECOSOC in coordinating international loan programs, Armeane Choksi, the World Bank's vice-president for human resources and operations policy, opposed "any altered relationship" between the United Nations and its specialized agencies, noting that this would "create another layer of bureaucracy." [10]

Proponents of the *Agenda*, however, contend that an altered relationship is needed to address the increasing dominance of the BWIs in directing national and international development policies. The South Center, for example, pointed out in its 1995 report entitled *The United Nations at the Crossroads* that the UN's research, policy formulation, and negotiating functions in such areas as international trade, development, finance, and monetary issues have diminished while the influence of the BWIs has steadily expanded. As a result, major policy concerns relating to foreign investment and the transfer of technology are not being adequately addressed in the international arena.[11]

It is a self-perpetuating myth that the BWIs are strictly financial institutions. Like the United Nations, they are subject to political pressures, mainly from the world's wealthiest nations, who are their major sources of lending capital. Since the 1970s the BWIs have taken an increasingly interventionist posture with regard to the domestic economic policies of the borrowing nations. In contrast, the BWIs have little control over the economic policies of the industrial nations, even though these same countries are also major debtors. It is true that the BWIs are concerned primarily with economic rather than social conditions. But advocates of increased UN control over the BWIs contend that the narrow economic focus of the BWIs is contributing to political, environmental, and social instability worldwide, and that a more central role for the United Nations would result in more balanced lending policies. According to the South Center, the opposition to a strong and dynamic United Nations is "political and profoundly ideological" and is largely concentrated in the nations whose economic elites prefer not to strengthen a forum in which their domestic and global policies can be challenged. Such criticism of the BWIs and sentiment that the United Nations should assume a greater role in managing the global economy were central themes at the March 1995 World Summit for Social Development (held in Copenhagen), which called for more "human-centered" development policies.

A more central role in the BWIs for the United Nations would result in more balanced lending policies.

Since 1947, when the BWIs officially became specialized agencies of the UN system, efforts to ensure that they would coordinate their activities with ECOSOC have proved fruitless due to IMF and World Bank resistance. BWI members actively participate in the activities of ECOSOC, including committee and subcommittee meetings, but UN committee members do not receive the same welcome at BWI meetings. In recent years, the representative of the secretary-general has been excluded from the biannual meetings of the World Bank's Interim Committee and Development Committee. While the IMF managing director and the World Bank president make annual addresses to the Economic and Social Council, UN leaders receive no invitation to address the BWIs. In other words, reciprocity is not a principle that guides the BWIs in their relationship with the United Nations.[12]

Also at issue is the relationship between the United Nations and the World Trade Organization, the successor to GATT. The conferees at the Bretton Woods meeting did propose the creation of the International Trade Organization (ITO) to promote and monitor the liberalization of global commerce. Not only was the ITO to reduce international trade barriers, but it was also to establish regulations regarding foreign investment, the protection of infant industries, and other development measures.

At the time, the U.S. Congress declined to authorize the United States to join such an organization, believing that it would infringe too heavily on U.S. sovereignty. As a substitute to the ITO, the capitalist nations established the multilateral trade accord called the General Agreement on Tariffs and Trade (GATT). At the conclusion of the Uruguay Round of GATT negotiations, the more than 120 members agreed to establish the World Trade Organization, thereby finally completing the triumvirate of global economic organizations envisioned at Bretton

Woods. In 1995 the General Assembly scheduled for discussion the UN's relationship with this new multilateral trade organization, which (like the other two BWIs) operates independently from ECOSOC and the UN's specialized economic development agencies. In the absence of a reform agenda by the less developed nations and because of the continuing resistance by wealthier capitalist nations to all attempts to change the structure of global economic relations, such coordination between the United Nations and the BWIs is unlikely.

Integrated Globalization

If the United Nations is to fulfill its mission to maintain global peace and to foster social and economic welfare, it must be given the authority and the resources to regulate the forces of economic globalization (mainly the TNCs). Yet, other important forces shaping globalization, such as the World Bank and the IMF, must also be controlled. In order to make them more accountable to development, the formal operations of the BWIs should be coordinated more closely with the work of the United Nations.[13]

Urgently needed is the formulation and enforcement of codes of conduct for transnational corporations that will make these powerful actors more accountable. The United Nations is the appropriate institution to develop codes of conduct in such areas as child labor, hazardous dumping, the public right-to-know about corporate plans and environmental practices, and the right to organize.[14] Effective enforcement of codes of conduct will depend largely on the strength of transnational citizen organizing and education efforts.

Closely associated with the need for corporate codes of conduct is the necessity of regulating or establishing an international regimen conducive to the regulation of global capital flows. Economic policies supported by the BWIs facilitate the unimpeded flow of capital, but this increasing mobility of capital is proving detrimental to national and regional development strategies and is leading to economic and political instability throughout the globe. Without a new UN capacity to monitor and coordinate international development, it is likely that the resulting economic polarization will further undermine global peace and prosperity. The United Nations has a vital role to play in integrating and regulating the diverse and too often destructive forces of economic globalization.

Chapter Seven

The Arms Connection

An oft-expressed rule of literary expression has it that a weapon introduced into the first act of a drama will be fired by the third. Yet in the drama of international affairs, the abundance of weapons on the world stage is not a pressing concern of the leading actors. For the most part, the world's leaders see weapons more as goods to be traded and political gifts to be disbursed than as instruments of war. This amazing disjuncture between fact and reason has survived the cold war. Today, as in the past, the imperative to increase national exports through arms production overrides concerns that sooner or later those exported weapons will be used.

There are two major reasons why arms control and disarmament are not high on the agenda of the United Nations. The first is the fact that the five permanent members of the Security Council (along with Germany) dominate the global weapons market. Any attempt to reduce the production and trade of conventional weapons would be a blow to their trade accounts. The second factor is the general reluctance on the part of the United Nations and its leading members to take measures that would regulate the international market. Business is business, and it should not be regulated or stopped, despite the bloody (and costly) repercussions of the arms trade.

The United Nations, through the IAEA and the NPT, has played a role in the control of nuclear weapons. But nonproliferation, while a step in the right direction, does not mean disarmament, and the control that is exerted is mainly to keep the nuclear weapons that do exist in the hands of the major nuclear powers, which also happen to be the five permanent members of the Security Council. This control by the "haves" creates resentment among the "have-nots." It also furthers the belief that having a nuclear weapons capacity is the true measure of global power and a nation's best defense.

Despite the efforts of the nuclear powers to keep nuclear weapons within their own exclusive domain, such nations as Israel, India, Pakistan, and North Korea may now have the capacity to detonate nuclear devices, along with a few new states of the former Soviet Union. Unfortunately, the end of the cold war did not spur the United States and other members of the nuclear club to move from a position of nonproliferation and nuclear arms control to total disarmament. As long as nuclear weapons exist, the threat of a nuclear conflagration remains.

Arms Sales Keep World at War

The hypocrisy of the Security Council's permanent members in acting as the guardians of global peace but continuing to insist on maintaining their nuclear weapons is further evident in their unwillingness to move to end the global arms trade in conventional weapons. A verbal commitment to maintaining global peace while readying countries for war may boost the trade accounts and the profits of arms merchants in the nuclear nations, but there are high costs when war does break out. In some cases, such as Somalia, the arms are even turned back on the nations that supplied them.

The permanent members of the Security Council are doubly responsible for the severity and longevity of many conflicts in the poorer nations. More than 80 percent of the conventional arms supplied to the poorer nations come from the same five countries that are supposedly the guardians of global peace.[1] Not only do the permanent Security Council members keep the poor nations armed and dangerous (both to their own populations and to their neighbors), but they also play a part in keeping these countries impoverished by encouraging the channeling of scarce funds into equipping their armed forces.[2] A UN report in 1982 that advocated "international disarmament for development" explicitly acknowledged this relationship, but the report was not accepted by the General Assembly because of cold war pressures.

The end of the cold war did little to alter the traditional U.S. approach to national security.

In the absence of an effective collective security environment, the birth of new nations in the last fifty years has resulted in the creation of new armies, which has increased the demand for weapons in the third world. Because few less developed nations produce their own weapons, poor countries account for a large portion—about 60 percent—of the world's weapons imports.[3]

Since the founding of the United Nations, governments have spent an estimated $30 trillion for military purposes. In the last 25 years, an estimated 250 million land mines have been manufactured.[4] Because of the widespread availability of weapons, an armed conflict can continue indefinitely. One has only to look at Central America, the former Yugoslavia, or Angola to see how the easy availability of arms fuels conflicts year after year.

Arms sales have been flourishing in the Middle East. Following the Persian Gulf War, which showcased new

UNICEF/93-1177/Horner

'Displaced' child sits atop remnant of Nicaragua's long civil war.

U.S. high-tech weaponry, the demand for U.S. weapons has dramatically increased. In the 1991-94 period the United States sold $43.9 billion in arms to Kuwait, Saudi Arabia, Israel, Turkey, and other countries in the Middle East.[5] According to defense analyst Michael Klare, "the unparalleled selling spree was viewed by the other major military suppliers as bestowing carte blanche on their own marketing activities." [6] Despite the U.S. government's stated commitment to promoting democracy, it supplies military regimes and dictatorships with the arms they use to repress their own populations and threaten neighbors. According to one estimate, 90 percent of the U.S. weapons that went to poor nations in 1993 went to nations that were not democracies.[7]

In Washington, the end of the cold war did little to alter the traditional U.S. approach to national security. Instead of using the collapse of its nemesis as an opportunity to shape an alternative vision of national security, the Pentagon insisted on maintaining a large military industrial complex capable of fighting two major wars simultaneously. This vision of national defense keeps economic resources tied up in the Pentagon. The continued commitment to large military expenditures has more to do with the domestic political need to appear strong on defense and to maintain the support of the military industrial complex than on any realistic evaluation of threats to U.S. security.

Chapter Eight

Paying the Bills

As the United Nations looks to its next fifty years, in addition to questions of identity and purpose it also faces a deepening financial crisis. The surge in peace operations since 1988 compounded an already serious problem of insufficient funding. Lack of funds have contributed to cutbacks in development programs and to a reluctance to undertake new peacekeeping missions.

The United Nations, including its specialized agencies (but excluding the World Bank, GATT, and the IMF) and its peace operations, has an annual budget of approximately $7 billion. The regular budget, which covers the operations of the UN's principal organs, was $1.35 billion in 1995. Peacekeeping cost $3.1 billion in 1994, while the specialized agencies have a combined budget of approximately $2 billion. Each month the United Nations needs approximately $400 million to meet the cost of its regular budget and peacekeeping operations. In an October 1994 report to the General Assembly by the secretary-general, it was noted that as of August 1994 the United Nations had $375 million on hand but owed approximately $1.7 billion to creditors.[1]

The General Assembly determines the UN's regular budget, and its Committee on Contributions assesses

Top Ten Assessments to UN's 1995 Regular Budget

Country	Percentage
United States	25.00
Japan	13.95
Germany	8.94
France	6.32
Russian Federation	5.68
Britain	5.27
Italy	4.79
Canada	3.07
Spain	2.24
Brazil	1.62
Total	**76.88%**

Source: UN Secretariat, *Status of Contributions as at 31 July 1995* (New York: United Nations, August 1995).

what member nations are obligated to contribute. Assessments are set according to a nation's ability to pay, although U.S. pressure in the early 1970s resulted in a contributions cap of 25 percent—the proportion of the UN's regular budget currently assessed to the United States. There is also a minimum assessment of 0.01 percent of the UN budget that ninety-four nations—more than one half of the total members—are obliged to pay annually.

Because of the great disparity between rich and poor nations, the UN's budget is paid mainly by the world's wealthier nations. The top ten contributors account for more than three-quarters of the regular UN budget, while the other 175 member nations cover the remaining one-quarter (Figure 8a). The African countries, the largest single geographical grouping of nations, together account for only 1.3 percent of the total UN budget.

Apart from the regular budget, nations are also assessed for the cost of UN peace operations. There is a different scale of assessments for peacekeeping that places a higher burden on the five permanent members of the Security Council.[2] These assessments pay for the cost of current peace missions, which means that when the United Nations undertakes a new mission it generally does not have the funds to cover the cost but relies, instead, on future assessments for each operation. This practice was called "financial bungee jumping" by former Undersecretary-General of Administration and Management Richard Thornburgh.[3]

Failure to pay the UN's assessments has been a mounting problem. At the start of 1995 accumulated arrears topped $2.4 billion, more than $1.3 billion of which was for peacekeeping. Only 75 member states had paid their assessments in full and 39 members had made no payments to the UN's regular budget in 1994. Today as arrearages have grown they also have become more concentrated. As of July 1995, 10 members accounted for 86 percent of the total amount outstanding to the UN regular budget (Figure 8b). Since 1986 the United States has been the UN's largest debtor, accounting for 60 percent of the UN's arrears in 1994. In addition to the continuing problem of arrears, the UN's financial stability is undermined by the practice of some nations, mainly the United States, of withholding a portion of their UN dues because of disagreement with particular UN programs.

When the United Nations undertakes a new mission it generally does not have the funds to cover the cost.

So acute was the financial crisis in the UN's 50th year that it explored the possibilities of borrowing money from the World Bank and of selling the debts of countries

Ten Largest UN Debtors

Regular		Peacekeeping	
United States	$527,154,431	United States	$647,623,365
South Africa	$61,115,320	Russian Fed.	$499,863,234
Ukraine	$52,578,602	Ukraine	$164,178,794
Brazil	$25,877,856	France	$82,653,237
Russian Fed.	$20,529,698	South Africa	$52,849,069
Belarus	$12,177,785	Belarus	$42,608,537
Iran	$11,541,449	Italy	$27,310,226
Yugoslavia*	$10,831,604	Georgia	$16,667,696
Kazakstan	$9,973,515	Iran	$13,343,382
Uzbekistan	$9,078,534	Brazil	$13,026,438
Total	**740,858,794**		**1,560,123,978**
Others	124,746,482	Others	114,916,900
Outstanding	**865,605,276**		**1,675,040,878**

Top 10 debtors as percentage of total outstanding:

86%	93%

* Serbia and Montenegro have been barred from taking up the former Yugoslavian seat at the United Nations and have to reapply, thus no assessments for Yugoslavia have been paid.
Source: UN Secretariat, *Status of Contributions as at 31 July 1995* (New York: United Nations, August 1995).

in arrears to private companies, which would then attempt to collect on the bad debts. Neither option was approved, but the United Nations was forced to dip into emergency peacekeeping funds to cover routine expenses. "I've never seen anything so precariously balanced at this scale," exclaimed Joseph E. Connor, the UN's new undersecretary-general of administration and management. "There's no capital and no reserves." After emptying the peacekeeping reserves, Connor griped that to keep the organization afloat his office had to use funds from new assessments to pay off past bills. "In the textbooks, it's called a Ponzi scheme," he told the *New York Times*.[4]

Arrears, and the now-common practice by nations of delaying payment of their annual assessments, are the chief causes of the UN's shaky financial condition. President Clinton, addressing the United Nations on the occasion of its 50th anniversary, focused instead on its "bureaucratic inefficiencies and outdated priorities." Like all old institutions, private or public, the United Nations can indeed be made more efficient and would benefit from an evaluation of its priorities, but such criticisms should be given in context. By one estimate, there are more civil servants in Wyoming (a state with only 450,000 people) than the 52,000 employed by the entire UN system.[5] The UN's budget, while not as trim as it could be, is relatively small, especially when considering that it is a system of agencies that responds to the peace, developmental, and humanitarian needs of a world of nearly six billion people.

Chapter Nine

Making the United Nations More Representative

To increase the UN's credibility and its effectiveness as an impartial international organization, the UN system must be more representative. Among the smaller, less developed nations, there is the belief that the current structure of the United Nations reinforces the inequality among states. This inequality is reflected not only in the formal structure—namely the preeminence of the Security Council—but also in the influence that the industrial nations, mainly the United States, have in financing, appointing the secretary-general, and selecting which operations to support.

Also raising the ire of those excluded from permanent membership in the Security Council are the structural insults that meetings are closed, decisions are made informally, and meeting minutes are not made public. Especially in Asia and Africa, there is the persistent criticism that the United Nations is a foreign policy instrument of the United States, whose influence extends far beyond its authority as a permanent member of the Security Council.[1] Economic and military power also translate into vote-buying power. It is well-known, for example, that the U.S. government rewards nations that follow its lead and punishes those that vote contrary to the U.S. position by increasing or decreasing aid or modifying trading rights. In a not entirely successful campaign to increase support for the U.S. positions in the United Nations, the Reagan administration initiated a policy that linked foreign aid to a country's UN voting record.

The United Nations represents the world's best hope for an institution that can guide international social and economic development while bringing peace to conflictive regions. Unlike other global institutions such as the World Bank and the World Trade Organization, the United Nations is more open and representative.

But the United Nations is hardly a perfect democracy. Indeed, it was never designed to be one. The challenge of those hoping to make the United Nations more representative will be to find a structure that both reflects the influence and responsibility of the world's most powerful nations and gives the less powerful nations an increased role in the UN's most important decisions.

One Country, One Vote

Even without reform, the structure of the United Nations is more democratic than the other leading international institutions. The smallest nations have a voice in the General Assembly, and UN proceedings are more open to public review. But there are obvious limitations to representative governance at the United Nations.

Within the General Assembly, where each nation has one vote, the main issue for larger nations like the United States is that smaller nations have as much voting power as larger ones and as those that contributed substantially more to the UN's budget. One of the UN's newest members, Andorra (admitted in 1993), has a population of only sixty thousand. Two of every three member states have a population of fewer than ten million.[2]

This system is particularly frustrating for the United States, which accounts for about one-quarter of the UN's budget, has only one vote, and usually finds itself in the minority. In keeping with its minority opinions about such matters as Israel, the United States votes "no" in the plenary sessions more than any other member nation. In 1991, the United States found itself among a minority of three or less in the General Assembly 34 of the 70 times it voted.[3] In the 1988-91 period, the U.S. coincidence with the majority position was never higher than 28 percent in any year and in one year fell to 15 percent.[4]

The United Nations is a state-centered system, not a people-centered one.

In the name of making the General Assembly more representative, some proposals advocate a weighted voting system whereby each nation would be given one vote but the more populous nations and the ones that contribute more to the UN budget would be given proportionately more voting power. One version of the weighted system, called the "Binding Triad" concept, would make General Assembly decisions binding in all matters (except the use of force) if proposals receive the affirmative votes of countries: 1) contributing two-thirds of the regular UN budget; 2) representing two-thirds of the world's population; and 3) comprising two-thirds of the member states.[5]

Proposals to establish weighted voting systems in the General Assembly usually receive more support from the world's largest nations, while the smaller states object, charging that the purpose and value of the United Nations is to offer an equal forum for all the world's countries. Many of world's smaller and less developed nations also contend that control of the Security Council by some of the world's most powerful states already puts less powerful countries in a disadvantaged place in the UN system.

President Clinton addresses the 48th session of the General Assembly.

Another criticism of the weighted voting system is that the representation is not democratic in that governments, not people, are represented by the ambassadors who vote in the General Assembly. The United Nations is a state-centered system, not a people-centered one. Giving more voting power to some governments, especially to those that are not political democracies, would not result in better representation of the people of those nations. Closely associated with the criticism of the world body as being state-centered are proposals from some internationalists that the United Nations should be restructured to include a global parliament whose members are directly chosen in UN-sponsored elections.

Since the governments that are members of the United Nations are not all democratic and are characterized by great differences in their legitimacy, a popularly elected "world citizens' assembly" that functioned alongside the General Assembly would make the United Nations more representative while opening the institution to greater grassroots input.[6] Examples of such transnational institutions based on direct elections include the European Parliament and the Central American Parliament. Other possibilities for making the UN more democratic and more accountable would be to give local governments, nongovernmental organizations, and churches observer status at the United Nations.

Any proposed reform of the General Assembly that would alter the present balance of power in the United Nations would likely aggravate tensions between the world's most powerful and less powerful countries. A change in the voting system would require a two-thirds majority. In theory, the less developed and smaller states could push through and block changes because of their superior numbers. But the votes of many governments are often determined by the financial, political, and even military influence of the most powerful nations. It is unlikely that there will be any effort to change the voting system of the General Assembly independent of proposals to restructure the Security Council, where the real power of the United Nations lies.

General Assembly resolutions on international affairs are nonbinding. Since many members have no immediate interest in the issues being debated on the floor, votes are commonly traded. The uncontroversial character of most General Assembly votes is indicated by the rising number of decisions that are adopted by consensus. In the 46th assembly there were 348 resolutions and decisions passed by the General Assembly—272 (78 percent) of which were approved by consensus.[7] Given the General Assembly's lack of real power and considering the potential political risks, it is unlikely that there will be any serious reform effort to change its voting system. Such an effort would have to come from a reform coalition within the General Assembly, probably led by the countries of the South, but there are still no signs of the emergence of such a strong and unified reform bloc.

This absence of a political platform of the world's poorer nations is not unrelated to the pragmatic acknowledgment of the power of the United States—its undisputed military might, its ideological supremacy, the importance of its market, and its control over international lending patterns. The dominance of the United States was reinforced by the accession to the General Assembly of more than a dozen new states of the former Soviet Union, all of whom have become dependent on U.S. aid, trade, and investment and routinely support the U.S. position.

Reforming the Security Council

The Security Council looks much like it did when the United Nations was founded—five permanent members with veto power at its core, and rotating members without veto power on its periphery. At the time of the UN's founding, giving permanent seats to the five powers that emerged victorious from World War II—the United States, Soviet Union, Great Britain, France, and China—reflected the reality of the global power structure, although by no means mirroring the world's population distribution. Fifty years later, the structure of the Security Council seems even more like an old boy's club, a vestige of post-World War II reality that no longer corresponds to the global division of power and wealth. As Michael Renner of the Worldwatch Institute noted, "Large parts of the world, containing two-thirds of humanity, have only temporary representation in the Council." [8]

The structure of the Security Council seems ever more like an old boy's club.

Since 1946 there has been just one change in the structure of the Security Council. In 1965, in recognition of the increasing membership of the United Nations (rising from 51 at its founding to 115), it was decided to increase the number of temporary members on the Security Council from six to ten. Although by 1995 membership had increased to 185, neither the number of permanent nor temporary members has changed in the intervening three decades.

The inclusion of Japan and Germany—the leading Axis powers defeated by the Allies in World War II and today the second and third largest contributors to the UN budget—would better reflect the new structure of global economic power. By the same logic, however, the permanent seats of France and Great Britain—and perhaps even the debilitated Russian Federation—would have to be reconsidered—a move that would be resisted bitterly by those countries, whose presence on the Security

Council is one of the few remaining symbols of their status as global powers.

For the Security Council to become a more credible and representative institution, its structure would also have to change to include permanent representatives from the world's populous and developing countries. Brazil, India, and South Africa would be likely candidates, but other nations such as Argentina, Pakistan, and Nigeria would likely contest those nominations or put forward their own candidacies. To address these concerns, some have proposed that the Security Council have regional seats, such as a European seat that would allow the European powers to rotate. But questions of inclusiveness would need to be considered here, too. Would, for example, Portugal rotate into a seat previously occupied by Germany, or would Pakistan consider itself represented through a regional seat occupied by its rival India?

Closely associated with proposals to change the size and composition of the Security Council is a discussion about whether proposed new members should enjoy the veto privilege. Currently, according to the UN Charter, the five permanent members of the Security Council can veto proposed UN actions relating to maintaining international peace and security. During the cold war, the veto—which was used 242 times—kept the Security Council gridlocked. With the demise of the bipolar world, the veto has rarely been used—only seventeen times between 1988 and September 1995. Indeed, most actions and resolutions in recent years are decided by consensus. According to New Zealand's Permanent Representative to the United Nations, this new effort to achieve consensus "gives a lot of power to even one member of the Council that wants to stand out on an issue." [9]

Nonetheless, there is some concern among reformers that extending the power of the veto to other nations would increase the risk that the UN role in maintaining international peace would again be stymied by Security Council vetoes. One possibility to reduce this risk would be to limit the veto power to Chapter VII affairs relating to peace enforcement (thereby excluding most peace operations, which do not involve armed conflict) and to regional agreements covered under Chapter VIII.[10] Generally among those advocating reform there is a sense that the veto power should be limited, not extended to new permanent members, and be gradually abolished. Of the five permanent members, however, only China has indicated that it would be willing to abolish the veto, although there is wider support for limiting the scope of Security Council vetoes.[11]

Any attempt to change the composition of the Security Council is fraught with problems and would likely lead to an entire restructuring of the United Nations. Proposals to include Germany and Japan as permanent, veto-empowered members of the Council would surely elicit vetoes by other members, especially Britain and France.

An expansion of the Security Council to better reflect current global divisions of power and population might make it a more representative institution, but there would be no guarantee that the new Council would be more effective. More members, especially those with veto power, could lead to a new round of factionalism and gridlock. To avoid such an eventuality, it has been proposed that Security Council decisions be required to gain the approval of a majority of members and the acquiescence of a preponderant majority of the permanent members (five of seven, for example, if the council were expanded). Besides facing the risk of a deadlocked Security Council, reforms to restructure the Council would also have to consider the possibility that restructuring could lead to a decision by a major nation to renounce its membership, thereby critically weakening the institution.

In its public diplomacy, the U.S. government has lent support to proposals to reconfigure the Security Council, publicly supporting the proposal that Japan and Germany be included as permanent members.[12] Such a move might help ease the financial burden on the United States by giving these economic powerhouses more of a stake in the United Nations, but it would exacerbate the control by the North. In contrast, the United States has not used its influence to advocate for a better North-South balance on the Security Council.

Unless the U.S. government takes action, itself, as the world's leading economic and military power, to carry through such restructuring, its support can be regarded as political posturing. Like other nations, the United States sees the United Nations as a means to further its own interests. Any measure to change the size and composition of the Security Council would likely necessitate amending the UN Charter and, as such, could open the way to widespread discussion about the overall structure and purpose of the United Nations.[13]

Not Just a Matter of Principle

More democracy and better accountability at the United Nations are needed to make it a more effective international institution. As it is, the UN's unbalanced power structure results in a skewed sense of purpose. Dominating the UN's agenda are the peace and security concerns of the United States, the organization's most powerful member. Pushed to the side are the developmental and humanitarian needs of the poorer, less influential nations. A more democratic United Nations—the result either of a series of reforms or of a new Charter—would increase the credibility of the institution. Such action could enable the United Nations to take more unified and effective steps to guarantee global peace and security and to address the intensifying social and environmental crises.

Conclusion

An Agenda for Change

The president of the United Nations Association of the United States of America (UNA-USA) in testimony before Congress in 1993 concluded that "the UN is on the verge either of a great leap forward or of a missed opportunity of tragic proportions."[1] Most U.S. citizens are generally supportive of the United Nations, and the Clinton administration has been a stronger advocate of multilateralism than previous, Republican administrations.

In the United States there is an absence of a compelling vision of the respective roles of the United Nations and the United States in forging a new world order. Those groups and politicians who do support a reformed and strengthened United Nations face the strong opposition of the political right, including those who regard any commitment to multilateralism as an attack on national sovereignty as well as those who regard the UN only as an instrument that can sometimes be tapped to further U.S. foreign policy goals.

Internationally, although there have been promising proposals regarding such issues as the reform of the Security Council and the creation of stand-by peacekeeping forces, there has not emerged any new overarching vision of the UN's role for the coming century.[2]

It appears that the United Nations will be left to enter the next century with the structure and directions that were only barely adequate for the present one.

New Millenium, New Vision

Despite all the criticism of the United Nations, especially from the right wing, there still exists in the United States and in societies around the world a deep reservoir of UN support. All the faultfinding about the United Nations has failed to undermine the essential support for the concept of an international institution concerned with maintaining global peace, improving the human condition, and making and upholding international law.

Although the UN states are far from reaching a consensus about how global affairs should be managed, there is an expanding realization, especially outside of government, that multilateral approaches are the only feasible way to address the numerous threats to global peace and well-being. NGOs, in particular, recognize that only by combining local activism with multilateral commitments can there be lasting solutions to such problems as environmental destruction, arms proliferation, population growth, the spread of infectious diseases, social disintegration, economic instability, and widening conflicts. It is also becoming more evident that, as trade, production, and finance are globalized and controlled by transnational corporations, international conventions and institutions like the United Nations are ever more needed to ensure that the environment is protected, cultures are preserved, and living conditions are improved.

During the first fifty years of the United Nations, considerable progress was made in establishing a place for multilateralism. As the world approaches a new millenium, it is time to make certain that the achievements of the past are not lost. We must begin to lay the groundwork for an expanded vision of how the world's united nations can solve their problems together.

A More Representative United Nations

Democratic reforms to make the United Nations more representative, less controlled by the United States, and more inclusive are essential if the world body is to become a stronger and more credible force in maintaining international peace and improving human welfare. At the top of an agenda for change for the United Nations in the next fifty years is a restructuring of the Security Council to make it more representative. Clearly, there are strong arguments for including Japan and Germany in the Security Council, given their economic power—although neither country has shown the inclination to parlay its economic might to gain global political influence. Before considering the claims of other Northern nations for membership, however, any change in the composition of the Security Council must first redress the problem of Northern domination by including more representation from the poorer and nonnuclear powers.

There is an expanding realization that multilateral approaches are the only feasible way to address the numerous threats to global peace.

The veto system needs reforming. One possibility would be to expand the council's permanent membership and require that council decisions on peacekeeping garner the assent of the large majority of these members.

If the Security Council were made more representative, it might also be possible to restructure the General Assembly to improve its credibility. Some sort of weighted voting system would address the concern that nations having small populations and economies have as much weight in the international assembly as the world's most populous and economically powerful ones. In any event, there needs to be better and more open communication between the General Assembly and the Security Council.

In keeping with the post-cold war limits of national sovereignty and the emergence of a new global society, the United Nations and member states should encourage increased participation in global affairs by NGOs, including churches, development groups, unions, and policy institutes. There should be more systematic involvement of NGOs, not just in humanitarian, developmental, and environmental affairs but also in peace and security issues. It has been repeatedly demonstrated that informal networks involving local governments, NGOs, and government agencies are often more effective in resolving conflicts than are formal negotiations. The United Nations should seek, then, to maximize the participation of nongovernmental entities.

National Sovereignty and Multilateralism

The main challenge to national sovereignty has been economic globalization, but the United Nations has also played an important role in asserting international law and principles in what were formerly the purely domestic affairs of nations. The parameters of national sovereignty are today less extensive than they were when the United Nations was founded. At the same time, however, the moral and practical limits of internationalism need to be acknowledged. International respect for the self-determination of peoples, especially when it leads to the destruction of existing states, should not be an operative principle of a new universalist agenda. Although perhaps not ideal, the existence of multiethnic and pluralistic nations is a better political option than a multitude of self-determined (but exclusive and dysfunctional) states.

While appeals to national sovereignty can be abused in allowing a nation to continue with impunity its abuses of the human and political rights of its inhabitants, the principle of national sovereignty can also help protect small nations against international bullies. The respect of national sovereignty would also allow individual nations to order their political and economic systems in ways that best serve the interests and needs of their citizens—without the interference of an oppressive international order. A clear and present danger is that such regional powers as the Russian Federation and the United States may use the erosion of the concept of national sovereignty to impose their own policies on weaker nations. Thus, a stronger United Nations is needed to ensure that future peacekeeping does not depend primarily on the unilateral operations of regional powers.

Yet another concern that arises from the waning of the national sovereignty principle is that intervention in the domestic affairs of nations may occur not based on some objective standard but rather according to determinations of the strategic interests of the world's most powerful nations. As Thomas Weiss, director of the Thomas J. Watson, Jr., Institute for International Studies, recently observed, "When conflicts are clearly regarded as challenges to the dominant political and economic order, intervention is more likely."[3] A more democratically structured United Nations would help guard against this skewed motivation for intervention.

With regard to maintaining international peace and security, the main focus of the United Nations should be on preventing and resolving disputes between nations, particularly in the cases of egregious territorial aggression. The full force of international diplomacy together with a well-targeted strategy of sanctions and embargoes should be brought to bear on conflicts before intervention is considered. In an increasingly interrelated world, international sanctions that exclude a nation from the international community are an increasingly powerful diplomatic weapon.

Intervention in domestic conflicts needs to be guided by predetermined standards, not by media attention (the so-called "CNN factor") or the narrow strategic interests of the great powers. As one analyst suggested, "The United Nations cannot intervene in all situations, and its decisions to intervene must therefore be based on objective criteria, balancing its long-term goals, its capabilities, and human need."[4] The extent of bloodshed, the righteousness of the cause, the feasibility of a negotiated solution, and the capability of UN peacekeeping forces all need to be considered by the Security Council after diplomatic measures have been exhausted before UN intervention is authorized. Moreover, it must be remembered that foreign intervention in domestic conflicts is an extremely risky and messy affair, as the experiences in Somalia, Bosnia, and Cambodia have illustrated.

Peacemaking, not warmaking, should be the UN's clear mission. Accordingly, the United Nations must exercise more control over peace enforcement actions that it has authorized. Although the Security Council did authorize member states to use all necessary means to expel Iraq from Kuwait, it is doubtful that all diplomatic means to stop the aggression were fully explored before the U.S.-led forces let loose the most intensive bombing campaign since World War II.

Peacekeeping

The United Nations could act more effectively as a peacekeeping organization if it enjoyed a more secure financial base from which to undertake peace operations. Fundamental to a more successful UN peacekeeping role is a stronger commitment to conflict prevention. If they are to detect potential conflicts, the Secretariat and the Security Council should have access to an intelligence unit that monitors tensions between nations and between subnational groups. A critical part of such an early warning system would be information from satellites about troop, weapons, and population movements and transfers. The French have proposed the creation of a satellite verification agency that would have access to data accumulated by national systems. The United States and other nations with satellite technology should make it available to the United Nations in the interests of strengthening the UN's collective security system.

The United Nations needs a secure communications center, training facilities, an operations center, and a common military doctrine.

Once warned of a breaking conflict, the United Nations should have trained mediators available to seek a peaceful settlement. These UN mediators would supplement the preventive diplomacy exercised by the secretary-general. The operative principle of such conflict-prevention initiatives should be that war represents the failure of politics.[5]

To be effective, UN peacekeeping needs to be restructured. As it is, UN peace operations are hampered by their ad hoc character, faulty logistics, absence of a central command, lack of joint training, and inadequate financing. To adequately oversee peace enforcement operations, the United Nations needs a secure communications center, training facilities, an operations center, and a common military doctrine. According to the former head of the UNA-USA organization, the United Nations also needs a "large group of military advisers at headquarters, prepositioned equipment, a more fully integrated logistics and command structure, and significant financial reserves on which to draw in fast-breaking contingencies."[6]

Every effort needs to be taken to dissuade nations and subnational groups from using military means to achieve their objectives or settle their differences with others. In addition to mediation and diplomacy, there should be better use of economic sanctions and more deployment of UN peacekeeping forces for the purpose of discouraging the initiation of hostilities. The placement of UN Blue Helmets on the Macedonia frontier is a model for preventive deployment.

The majority recommendation of the United States Commission on Improving the Effectiveness of the United Nations that a UN rapid-reaction force be established should be considered. The Commission also suggested, in accordance with Articles 43 and 47 of the UN Charter, that the United States should negotiate stand-by arrangements with the United Nations that would earmark national troops and facilities for UN service.[7] A variation on this proposal would be the creation of a two-tiered system, the first tier consisting of a 10,000-person unit of blue helmets recruited by the United Nations that could be rapidly deployed to prevent conflicts from erupting and to monitor cease-fires. For peace enforcement missions, the United Nations would have stand-by arrangements with member nations in which certain troops would be specially designated and trained for UN operations and could be rapidly deployed if hostilities broke out.[8]

In principle, improvement of the multilateral capacity to make, keep, and build peace around the world should be supported. But to ensure that this multilateral peacekeeping force would not be the exclusive instrument of the major powers, there needs to be structural reform at the United Nations to guarantee that decisionmaking power is more broadly shared. Given the UN's lack of resources, its incapacity to lead effective peacekeeping missions throughout the world, and persistent concerns that the world body is mainly an instrument of the major powers, the United Nations should, for the time being, focus more on preventive diplomacy and classical peacekeeping than on more complicated and risky peace enforcement missions, especially in civil conflicts where there is no consensus about the UN's role.

Economic Sanctions

Closely related to peacekeeping and disarmament is the need for a better policy of economic sanctions. Especially when combined with mediation and preventive diplomacy, sanctions can play a very effective role in preventing and ending conflicts. But there does not exist a cohesive policy for multilateral sanctions. As a result, sanctions are often ineffective and selectively applied. Furthermore, they frequently unfairly affect neighboring nations and disproportionately burden the poor while elites feel relatively little impact. Scholars at the Joan B. Kroc Institute for International Peace Studies at the University of Notre Dame have formulated a set of criteria for sanctions that should be considered as a basis for a UN economic sanctions policy. They recommend:

- Exemption of humanitarian goods, especially food and medicine;
- Severe enforcement measures, including secondary boycotts, against nations that do not fully comply with an international system of sanctions;
- Use of sanctions only against nations that have violated basic norms of international law, including aggression, acquiring weapons of mass destruction, and gross human rights violations;
- Targeting political and military elites as much as possible;
- Compensation for countries whose economies are most burdened by compliance with the sanctions.[9]

Development and Peace

There can be no lasting peace without economic and social justice. Attempts to curtail the work of UN development agencies need to be opposed. Instead, these agencies should be given an increased role in addressing such problems as human rights abuses, economic polarization, and the unavailability of such basic goods as food, education, housing, and health care.

Reforms to the United Nations should not succumb to narrow definitions of peace and international security. It should be remembered, as stated in Article 55 of the UN Charter, that the purpose of the United Nations is to "promote higher standards of living, full employment, and conditions of economic and social progress and development." Ideally, the United Nations, as the world's most representative institution, would be given new authority over the world's multilateral financial and trade institutions, namely the World Bank, the IMF, and the World Trade Organization. Narrowly focused lending and trade organizations commonly clash with and subvert efforts to shape equitable development policies and foster participatory societies. An oversight role by the United Nations would help ease North-South tensions and could help avert new conflicts among the industrialized nations over shares of global trade and investment.

U.S. foreign policy needs to give more weight to its long-term interests in shaping a peaceful, prosperous, and just world.

Heightened attention to global social and economic problems should be accompanied by an understanding that environmental deterioration is also a major threat to the peace and security of the world's nations. Short of a revitalized United Nations assuming an oversight role regarding global development programs—an unlikely possibility, at least in the short and medium terms—the increased involvement of NGOs in global affairs may help curb the power and influence of the global financial and trading organizations.

Some 114,000 children were separated from their families by the civil war in Rwanda.

International Law

Respect for international law is fundamental to a peaceful, just world order. The World Court needs to be better funded and staffed; but if it is to fulfill its potential, all the UN members, particularly the world's most powerful nations, must accept its compulsory jurisdiction. At least fifty nations have agreed to abide by the verdicts of the Court. By not doing so, the United States has weakened the authority of international law and the World Court. Proposals to establish an International Criminal Court to hear cases of individual violations of humanitarian law, such as participation in genocide, would obviate the need for the ad hoc creation of special tribunals, as in the cases of Rwanda and the former Yugoslavia. A more active World Court and the proposed International Criminal Court would help strengthen and define international norms.

The U.S. Role

The UN structure—with most power resting in the Security Council—renders it a less-than-egalitarian institution. In addition, the dominance of the United States, particularly since the crumbling of the Soviet bloc, makes the United Nations more hierarchical than democratic. In any discussion of UN reform, the fundamental role of the United States in financing, directing peacekeeping operations, and exercising global leadership must be recognized, evaluated, and to some degree accepted as the reality of global affairs.

Reforms, however, are needed to ensure that the United Nations does not function, particularly in the area of peacekeeping, solely as an instrument of U.S. foreign policy. Measures that might help reduce the U.S. influence include a restructuring of the Security Council, the creation of a permanent UN peacekeeping center and rapid deployment force, and a reduction in the proportion of U.S. assessments. In this regard, proposals from Secretary-General Boutros-Ghali and others have called for lowering the maximum assessment from 25 percent to 15-20 percent.

Another important element in reducing the perception that the United Nations is simply a U.S. foreign policy tool would be the formulation of a more enlightened U.S. foreign policy—one that accepted the role of the United States as a global leader. Toward this end, U.S. foreign policy would need to give more weight to the concerns of other nations and to the long-term interests of the United States in shaping a peaceful, prosperous, and just world. An enforced code of conduct for transnational corporations, for example, would be in the common interest of both the industrialized and less developed countries. Moreover, it is essential that the United States work toward the institution of an international rule of law that no nation could freely violate, as the United States has repeatedly done in the past by its policies toward Cuba, Nicaragua, Palestine, Panama, and others.

To uphold the rule of law at the international level and thereby strengthen the United Nations, the United States must agree to accept the compulsory jurisdiction of the World Court and not consider itself above international law. The United States should clear its arrears and set an international example by promptly paying its annual assessments.

The process of reformulating U.S. foreign policy is long overdue. Not only would such a process lead to a more constructive role for the United States in the United Nations, but it would also help U.S. citizens better understand and appreciate the many ways that foreign policy and domestic policy intersect. In its position as a global leader, the U.S. government should look beyond the narrow and ultimately destructive tenets of a neoliberal world order shaped primarily by competing marketing and production strategies to one in which the common interests of all nations are fundamental. By striving more for the long-term political and economic stability of the world order, the United States would gain new respect internationally while benefiting from a world less torn by economic and political strife.

References

Chapter One

1. The first General Assembly decided to locate the permanent head-quarters in the United States. John D. Rockefeller offered a gift of $8.5 million to purchase land on the banks of the East River. Today there is a cluster of four buildings: the General Assembly Building, the Secretariat Building, the Conference Building, and the Dag Hammarskjold Library. Total cost of construction was approximately $67 million, of which $65 million was financed by an interest-free loan from the United States. The Dag Hammarskjold Library, built at a cost of $6.6 million, was a gift of the Ford Foundation.

2. Stephen Schlesinger, "Cryptoanalysis for Peacetime: Codebreaking and the Birth and Structure of the United Nations," *Cryptologia,* 19 (3), July 1995. Also see Schlesinger, "The UN at 50: Will the US Go it Alone?" *The Nation*, May 15, 1995, p. 686.

3. The cold war was the main constraint to UN peacekeeping, but it should not be forgotten that the spheres of interest defined by colonialism, such as France's interests in Algeria and Vietnam, also narrowed the operating room for the United Nations.

4. Richard Falk, from proceedings of the 87th Annual Meeting of the American Society of International Law, March 31-April 3, 1993, p. 422.

Chapter Two

1. It was not until 1971 that the People's Republic of China was authorized to fill the China seat on the Security Council, even though the revolution had triumphed in 1949. The United States voted against admitting the communist state of China in place of the largely discredited Taiwanese government of Chiang Kai-shek, but was outvoted in the General Assembly.

2. It is interesting to note that Western Europe is defined not by geography but by cold war politics in that Canada, Australia, and New Zealand are included in the Western European region for the purposes of Security Council rotation.

3. Cited in Abba Eban, "The UN Idea Revisited," *Foreign Affairs*, 74 (5) (September/October 1995), p. 43.

4. With the inclusion of the People's Republic of China in 1971, the United Nations could rightfully claim to be a universalist institution. Nonetheless, there are a few countries, such as Switzerland, Nauru, and Tonga, that have not become members. Taiwan, which maintains that it should hold the China seat, is not a member. The Holy See (or Vatican) is not a member. Other entities, such as Serbia, Western Sahara, Palestine, and Northern Cyprus, also remain outside the United Nations either because the United Nations does not recognize their credentials (as in the case of Serbia) or because they do not maintain effective governmental control over their territories. Most of these nonmember states and territorial entities do, however, participate in the UN's specialized agencies.

5. The recent exception to this rule was the 1992 refusal by the General Assembly to recognize the credentials of the Federal Republic of Yugoslavia (Serbia and Montenegro) as the rightful successor of the former Socialist Federal Republic of Yugoslavia.

6. The First Committee addresses political and security issues, while economic and financial issues are discussed in the Second Committee, social issues in the Third Committee, territorial and trusteeship issues in the Fourth Committee, administrative and budgetary issues in the Fifth Committee, and legal issues in the Sixth Committee.

7. The institutional sexism in the Secretariat has come under increased fire, since women hold only approximately 4 percent of the senior policy positions in the agency.

8. The *New Internationalist* compared the salaries of the secretary-general, assistant secretary-general, and lowest professional-grade salaries of the United Nations against the president, department director, and general economist of the World Bank. In every case the salary of the UN employee was significantly lower than a similar position in the World Bank. Chris Brazier, "Winds of Change," *New Internationalist*, December 1994, p. 7.

9. Amos Yoder, *The Evolution of the United Nations System* (New York: Crane Russak, 1989), p. 134.

10. Territories that have never been under UN trusteeship, such as Puerto Rico, remain a concern of the United Nations. The UN Charter stipulates that nations responsible for administering territories accept the responsibility of maintaining the interests of the citizens in all decisionmaking; ensuring political, social, economic, and educational advancement; and permitting the citizens progressive development towards self-determination. Each year the non-self-governing territories are considered by the UN's Special Committee on the Situation with Regard to the Implementation of the Declaration on the Granting of Independence to Colonial Countries and Peoples (Committee of 24 or C-24).

11. Phyllis Bennis, *Calling the Shots: How Washington Dominates Today's UN* (New York: Olive Branch Press, 1996), p. 6, citing Schlesinger, "Cryptoanalysis for Peacetime," p. 224.

12. Michael H. Shuman and Hal Harvey, *Security Without War: A Post-Cold War Foreign Policy* (Boulder: Westview Press, 1993), p. 158.

13. UNICEF, *State of the World's Children* (Oxford: Oxford University Press, 1996).

14. Richard Falk, "Appraising the UN at 50: The Looming Challenge," *Journal of International Affairs*, 48 (2), Winter 1995.

15. This section on NGO involvement in the UN origins draws largely from Cecelia Lynch, "The Birth of the United Nations: The Importance of Domestic Legitimization," Draft manuscript for an

edited volume, *The United Nations at Fifty: Issues and Opportunities* (forthcoming). See also Dorothy B. Robins, *Experiment in Democracy: The Story of U.S. Citizen Organizations in Forging the Charter of the United Nations* (Minneapolis: Institute for Agriculture and Trade Policy, 1995).

16. Other groups were also involved in peace issues during the period of the UN formation, including the Women's International League for Peace and Freedom, Church Peace Union, National Council for Prevention of War, and such pacifists groups as the Fellowship of Reconciliation and the American Friends Service Committee (AFSC).

17. Lynch, "The Birth of the United Nations." See also Dorothy B. Robins, *Experiment in Democracy*.

Chapter Three

1. Robert W. Gregg, *About Face?: The United States and the United Nations* (Boulder: Lynne Rienner Publishers, 1993), p. 9.

2. Daniel Patrick Moynihan, *A Dangerous Place* (Boston: Little, Brown, & Company, 1978); Walters' statement is cited in S. Nihal Singh, "Using the UN Again," *World Press Review*, Novemeber 1990.

3. E. Gross, *Foreign Policy Bulletin*, September 15, 1954, cited in Geoff Simons, *The United Nations: A Chronology of Conflict* (New York: St. Martin's Press, 1994), p. 84.

4. Robert E. Riggs and Jack C. Plano, *The United Nations: International Organization and World Politics* (Chicago: Dorsey Press, 1988), p. 86.

5. Bennis, *Calling the Shots*, p. 235.

6. Tony Smith, *The Pattern of Imperialism* (New York: Cambridge University Press, 1981), p. 3.

7. Undersecretary of State for International Organizations, John Bolton, speaking at the Global Structures Convocation, Washington, DC, February 1994, cited in Bennis, *Calling the Shots*, p. xvi.

8. Michael Renner, *Remaking UN Peacekeeping: U.S. Policy and Real Reform*, Briefing Paper 17 (Washington, DC: National Commission

for Economic Conversion and Disarmament, November 1995).

9. The large U.S. assessment for peacekeeping is not paralleled by a large commitment of U.S. troops to peace missions. In 1993, U.S. troops accounted for 3.6 percent of total UN peacekeeping troop commitments. This dropped to 1.3 percent in 1994 after the U.S. contingent left Somalia and rose again to 5.4 percent in 1995 as a result of the Haiti mission. As of September 30, 1995, the U.S. ranked fourth in troop contributions, following the United Kingdom, France, and Pakistan. More than two-thirds of its 3,239 troops were stationed in Haiti, a country of special interest because of its proximity to and flow of refugees into the United States. If those troops, most of whom were left over from the U.S. occupation, were not counted, the United States would have ranked 18th in troop contributions.

10. United Nations, "Monthly Summary of Troop Contributions to Peacekeeping Operations as of 30 September 1995."

11. Phyllis Bennis, "Command and Control: Politics and Power in the Post-Cold War United Nations," in Phyllis Bennis and Michel Moushabeck, eds., *Altered States: A Reader in the New World Order* (New York: Olive Branch Press, 1993). Also see Bennis, *Calling the Shots*, pp. 31-3.

12. The U.S. assessment for peacekeeping rose from 30.4 percent to 31.7 percent following the collapse of the Soviet Union, but the United States refused to recognize the increase.

13. Renner, *Remaking UN Peacekeeping*, p. 17.

14. Ibid., p. 16.

15. These are 1994 figures, calculated from U.S. defense and national budget figures from the *Congressional Quarterly Alert* and from a listing of U.S. contributions to the United Nations found in various Congressional Research Service Issue Briefs.

16. "United Nations: 50 Years of Ups and Downs," *Newsweek*, October 30, 1995.

17. Burton Yales Pines, ed., *A World Without a U.N.* (Washington, DC: Heritage Foundation, 1985), p. xix.

Chapter Four

1. Victoria K. Holt, *Briefing Book on Peacekeeping: The U.S. Role in United Nations Peace Operations* (Washington, DC: Council for a Livable World Education Fund, March 1995), p. 1. This section on peacekeeping draws largely on the above report.

2. Project on Peacekeeping and the United Nations, "Current U.N. Peacekeeping Operations and U.S. Troop Levels" (Washington, DC: Council for a Livable World Education Fund, August 31, 1995).

3. Joseph S. Nye, Jr, "What New World Order?" *Foreign Affairs*, Spring 1992, p. 84.

4. Stanley R. Sloan, "Peacekeeping and Conflict Management Activities: A Discussion of Terminology" (Washington, DC: Congressional Research Service, November 26, 1993).

5. Boutros Boutros-Ghali, *An Agenda for Peace: Preventive Diplomacy, Peacemaking, and Peacekeeping* (New York: United Nations, June 17, 1992).

6. The missions and their start dates are as follows: UN Truce Supervision Organization (UNTSO) 1948; UN Military Observer Group in India and Pakistan (UNMOGIP) 1949; UN Peacekeeping Force in Cyprus (UNFICYP) 1964; UN Disengagement Observer Force (UNDOF) 1974; UN Interim Force in Lebanon (UNIFIL) 1978.

7. Holt, *Briefing Book*, p. 6.

8. A statement from a Boutros-Ghali press conference cited by Phyllis Bennis in her statement at the Reforming the Security Council conference, New York City, May 23, 1994.

9. UN Press Release SG/SM/4560, April 24, 1991.

10. See, for example, Chandra Muzaffar, *Human Rights and the New World Order* (Penang: Just World Trust, 1993). According to the author, the "centers of power in the North have narrowed the meaning of human rights in order to perpetuate their dominance." Instead of considering cultural, social, and economic rights, the focus in the North is on civil and political rights, argues the author.

11. For an excellent overview of the issues concerning UN involvement in national conflicts, see Thomas G. Weiss, ed., *The United Nations and Civil Wars* (Boulder: Lynne Rienner Publishers, 1995).

12. A survey by the Henry Stimson Center in Washington, DC, found that of the 77 countries that had contributed personnel to peace missions in 1993, only 8 provided a high level of peacekeeping training for their soldiers (Austria, Britain, Canada, Denmark, Finland, Ireland, Norway, and Sweden), while 15 others, including the United States, provided only moderate training. Barry M. Blechman and J. Mathew Vaccaro, *Training for Peacekeeping: The United Nations' Role*, Report No. 12 (Washington, DC: Henry L. Stimson Center, July 1994).

13. In 1993, voluntary and regular budget contributions accounted for only $5.5 million and $37.8 million, respectively, of the combined cost of peace operations that year.

14. When assessing poorer nations, the UN makes adjustments for factors unaccounted for in its general formula. These factors include the presence of wars, natural disasters, and anomalies in the available statistical information. To make up for the deficit due to the adjustments of the poorer groups, Security Council members have been assessed at approximately 27 percent above the baseline scale. See GAO, *United Nations: How Assessed Contributions for Peacekeeping Operations are Calculated*, August 1994, p. 11.

15. Renner, *Remaking UN Peacekeeping*, p. 5.

16. UN Secretariat, *Status of Contributions as of 30 November 1995*.

Chapter Six

1. For an overview of the UN's economic institutions and related reform initiatives see Lowell D. Ashby, *The United Nations' Economic Institutions and the Need for Restructuring* (Washington, DC: The Center for UN Reform Education, November 1991).

2. The New International Economic Order (NIEO) was proposed by the nations of the South in 1974 to reform the global economic system in ways that would open up the markets of industrialized nations to imports from less developed countries, increase the

terms of trade for those less developed nations that depended on commodity exports, reduce the debt burden of poor countries, and facilitate technology transfer to nonindustrialized nations. Although some critics on the left argued that the NIEO simply represented an adjustment in global capitalism, many program supporters hoped the reforms would substantially alter the structure of the global economy and thereby result in a just and equitable system of international economic relations. On the right, the NIEO was viewed as a symbol of the way the United Nations was being used to undermine the liberal international economic order, and it sparked a new wave of opposition to the United Nations, especially within the United States.

3. Richard Falk, "Appraising the UN at 50: The Looming Challenge," *Journal of International Affairs*, 48 (2), Winter 1995.

4. The Group of 77 (G77) emerged during the UN Conference on Trade and Development in 1964. It was not, however, until the onset of the New International Economic Order (NIEO) negotiations in the 1970s that the G77 became a prominent force. Although still known as the G77, the group currently includes more than 120 nations.

5. Chakravarthi Raghavan, "United Nations: UNCTAD Gets TNCs and Science and Technology Work," *Third World Network Features*, March 10, 1993.

6. Martin Khor, "The UN should Lead on Global Economic Issues," *Third World Network Features*, May 15, 1995.

7. Gerard Piel, "Globalopolies," *The Nation*, May 18, 1992; Ian Williams, "Why the Right Loves the U.N.," *The Nation*, April 13, 1992.

8. Martin Khor, "Need to Coordinate UN, World Bank, IMF Policies," *Third World Network Features*, March 28, 1995.

9. Martin Khor, "The UN Should Lead."

10. Martin Khor, "World Bank Insists on Distancing Itself from UN," *Third World Network Features*, March 28, 1995.

11. Cited in Chakravarthi Raghavan, "The United Nations at the Crossroads," *Third World Network Features*, May 22, 1995.

12. Alejandro Teitelbaum, "The United Nations and the Bretton Woods Institutions," *Third World Network Features*, Sept. 7, 1994.

13. For a discussion of these issues see the Stanley Foundation, *United Nations-Bretton Woods Collaboration: How Much is Enough?*, Report of the 26th UN Issues Conference, Convened at Arden House, Harriman, NY, February 24-26, 1995; and Haq Mahbub Ul, et al., eds., *The UN and the Bretton Woods Institutions: New Challenges for the 21st Century* (New York: St. Martin's Press, 1995).

14. Efforts to establish corporate codes of conduct were inspired by the successful campaign to make Nestlé restrict the marketing of its infant formula. The Sullivan principles for corporations doing business in the apartheid state of South Africa, and efforts by the Coalition for Justice in the Maquiladoras to hold U.S.-Mexico border factories to a code of conduct are other examples of campaigns to regulate TNC behavior.

Chapter Seven

1. Vanessa Baird, "Lethal Lies," *New Internationalist*, Nov. 1994.

2. Jacques Fontanel, "Investing in Peace," *UNESCO Courier*, October 1993, p. 20.

3. Michael Renner, *Critical Juncture: The Future of Peacekeeping*, Paper #114 (Washington, DC: Worldwatch Institute, 1993), pp. 17-8.

4. Ibid., p. 23.

5. Jeff Cole and Sarah Lubman, "Bombs Away: Weapons Merchants Are Going Great Guns in Post-Cold War Era," *Wall Street Journal*, January 28, 1994.

6. Michael T. Klare, "Adding Fuel to the Fire: The Conventional Arms Trade in the 1990s," in Daniel C. Thomas and Klare, eds., *World Security: Challenges for a New Century* (New York: St. Martin's Press, 1994), p. 136.

7. Cynthia McKinney and Caleb Rossiter, "It's Time the U.S. Stopped Boomerang Arms Sales," *Christian Science Monitor*, May 23, 1995, p. 19.

Chapter Eight

1. United States Department of State, *United States Participation in the United Nations: A Report by the President to Congress for the Year 1994* (Washington, DC: U.S. Government Printing Office, 1995), p. 205.

2. Developed nations are asssesed at the same rate as that of the regular UN budget, while less developed nations are assessed 10 percent less, and least developed nations are assessed 20 percent less than the regular budget rate. Permanent members of the Security Council are assessed higher to cover the remaining costs.

3. Quoted in "Bungee Jumping at the UN," *New York Times*, March 11, 1993.

4. Christopher S. Wren, "The UN's Master Juggler," *New York Times*, December 8, 1995.

5. Erskine Childers, "Foreword," in Bennis, *Calling the Shots*, p. x.

Chapter Nine

1. Richard Falk, "Appraising the UN at 50: The Looming Challenge," *Journal of International Affairs* 48 (2), Winter 1995.

2. United States Commission on Improving the Effectiveness of the United Nations, *Defining Purpose: The UN and the Health of Nations: Final Report of the United States Commission on Improving the Effectiveness of the United Nations* (Washington, DC: U.S. Government Printing Office, 1993), p. 34.

3. United States Department of State, *Voting Practices in the United Nations: 1991* (Washington, DC: Department of State Publications, 1992), p. 7.

4. Ibid., p. 32.

5. Richard Hudson, "Should there be a Global Parliament? What is the Binding Triad?" in Walter Hoffmann, ed., *A New World Order: Can it Bring Security to the World's People?* (Washington, DC: World Federalist Association, 1991). Hudson, the director of the Center for War/Peace Studies in New York, also proposes that no one nation contribute more than 15 percent of the UN budget, a measure that would reduce the influence of the United States.

6. This proposal is discussed by Ron Glossop, "Should there be a UN Parliamentary Assembly and/or Direct Popular Election of UN Delegates?" in Hoffmann, ed., *A New World Order*.

7. United States Department of State, *Voting Practices*, p. 63.

8. Michael Renner, *Critical Juncture*, p. 53.

9. Statement of Colin Keating at the Reforming the Security Council conference hosted by the Global Policy Forum and the International NGO Network on Global Governance, New York City, May 23, 1994.

10. See, for example, United States Commission on Improving the Effectiveness of the United Nations, *Defining Purpose*, p. 72.

11. Michael Renner, *Critical Juncture*, p. 54.

12. The Clinton administration, however, has not stated whether Japan and Germany should be given the same veto as other permanent members. Ambassador Albright has stated that the United States would not insist that the two countries revise their constitutions to allow their armies to participate in distant peace operations, suggesting instead that they could help with logistical and medical support.

13. Article 108 of the UN Charter stipulates that Charter amendments require the approval of two-thirds of the General Assembly members and must be ratified by all the permanent members of the Security Council.

Conclusion

1. Edward C. Luck, "Strengthening UN Management for a New Era," Testimony before the Subcommittee on Terrorism, Narcotics, and International Operations of the Senate Foreign Relations Committee, June 9, 1993.

2. For an overview of proposed UN reforms see Donald J. Puchala, "Outsiders, Insiders, and UN Reform," *The Washington Quarterly*, Autumn 1994.

3. Thomas G. Weiss, "The United Nations and Civil Wars," *The Washington Quarterly*, Autumn 1994, pp. 139-59.

4. Elizabeth Riddell-Dixon, "The United Nations and the Gulf War," *International Journal*, Spring 1994, p. 254.

5. Shuman and Harvey, *Security Without War*.

6. Luck, "Strengthening UN Management."

7. Already some sixty countries have begun the process of designating and training stand-by noncombatant personnel that will be on-call for peacekeeping service.

8. Two-tiered proposal from Renner, *Critical Juncture*.

9. David Cortright, "Used Well, Economic Sanctions Can Work to Resolve Conflicts," *The Truth*, July 16, 1995.

Glossary

CTC	Center on Transnational Corporations
ECOSOC	UN Economic and Social Council
ECOWAS	Economic Community of West African States
FAO	UN Food and Agriculture Organization
GATT	General Agreement on Tariffs and Trade
IAEA	International Atomic Energy Agency
IBRD	International Bank for Reconstruction and Development (World Bank)
ICAO	International Civil Aviation Organization
IDA	International Development Association
IFAD	International Fund for Agricultural Development
IFC	International Finance Corporation
ILO	International Labor Office
IMF	International Monetary Fund
IMO	International Maritime Organization
INSTRAW	International Research and Training Institute for the Advancement of Women
ITU	International Telecommunication Union
MIGA	Multilateral Investment Guarantee Agency
NGLS	UN Non-Governmental Liaison Service
NGO	Nongovernmental Organization
NPT	Nuclear Non-Proliferation Treaty
OAS	Organization of American States

OAU	Organization of African Unity
PLO	Palestine Liberation Organization
UN	United Nations
UNCHS	UN Center for Human Settlements
UNCTAD	UN Conference on Trade and Development
UNDP	United Nations Development Program
UNEP	United Nations Environment Program
UNESCO	UN Educational, Scientific, and Cultural Organization
UNFPA	United Nations Population Fund
UNHCR	Office of the UN High Commissioner for Refugees
UNICEF	UN Children's Fund
UNIDO	UN Industrial Development Organization
UNIFEM	UN Development Fund for Women
UNITAR	UN Institute for Training and Research
UNRWA	UN Relief and Works Agency for Palestine Refugees in the Near East
UNU	UN University
UPU	Universal Postal Union
WFC	World Food Council
WHO	World Health Organization
WIPO	World Intellectual Property Organization
WMO	World Meteorological Organization
WTO	World Trade Organization

Selected Bibliography

Phyllis Bennis, *Calling the Shots: How Washington Dominates Today's U.N.* (New York: Olive Branch Press, 1996).

Chris Brazier, "Winds of Change," *The New Internationalist* No. 262.

Marjorie Ann Brown, *United Nations Peacekeeping: Issues for Congress*, CRS Report for Congress (Washington, DC: Congressional Research Service, 1995).

Erskine Childers with Brian Urquhart, *Renewing the United Nations System* (Uppsala: Dag Hammarskjold Foundation, 1994).

Roger A. Coate, ed., *U.S. Policy and the Future of the United Nations* (New York: The Twentieth Century Fund Press, 1994).

Richard Falk, Samuel Kim, and Saul Mendlovitz, eds., *The United Nations and a Just World Order* (Boulder: Westview Press, 1991).

Richard Falk, "Appraising the U.N. at 50: The Looming Challenge," *Journal of International Affairs* 48 (2), Winter 1995.

General Accounting Office, *Peace Operations: Information on U.S. and U.N. Activities*, GAO/NSIAD-95-102BR (Washington, DC: Government Printing Office, February 1995).

Robert W. Gregg, *About Face?: The United States and the United Nations* (Boulder: Lynne Rienner Publishers, 1993).

Victoria K. Holt, *Briefing Book on Peacekeeping: The U.S. Role in United Nations Peace Operations* (Washington, DC: Council for a Livable World Education Fund, 1995).

Mark Lowenthal, *Peacekeeping in Future U.S. Foreign Policy*, CRS Report for Congress (Washington, DC: Congressional Research Service, 1994).

Daniel Patrick Moynihan, *A Dangerous Place* (Boston: Little, Brown & Company, 1978).

James A. Paul and Jan Lönn, eds., *Reforming the Security Council*, Proceedings of a Conference (New York: Global Policy Forum and the International NGO Network on Global Governance, 1994).

Michael Renner, *Critical Juncture: The Future of Peacekeeping*, Paper #114 (Washington, DC: Worldwatch Institute, 1993).

Michael Renner, *Remaking UN Peacekeeping: U.S. Policy and Real Reform*, Briefing Paper 17 (Washington, DC: National Commission for Economic Conversion and Disarmament, November 1995).

Adam Roberts and Benedict Kingsbury, eds., *United Nations, Divided World: The UN's Roles in International Relations* (Oxford: Clarendon Press, 1993).

Michael H. Shuman and Hal Harvey, *Security Without War: A Post-Cold War Foreign Policy* (Boulder: Westview Press, 1993).

Geoff Simons, *The United Nations: A Chronology of Conflict* (New York: St. Martin's Press, 1994).

United States Commission on Improving the Effectiveness of the United Nations, *Defining Purpose: The UN and the Health of Nations: Final Report of the United States Commission on Improving the Effectiveness of United Nations* (Washington, DC: Government Printing Office, 1993).

United States Department of State, *United States Participation in the United Nations: A Report by the President to Congress for the Year 1994* (Washington, DC: U.S. Government Printing Office, 1995).

Thomas G. Weiss, ed, *The United Nations and Civil Wars* (Boulder: Lynne Rienner Publishers, 1995).

Appendix 1

Top 100 Economic Units, 1993*

(US$ millions)

Rank	Unit	Net Sales or GNP
1	USA	6,259,889
2	Japan	4,214,204
3	Germany	1,910,760
4	France	1,251,689
5	Italy	991,3867
6	United Kingdom	819,038
7	Spain	478,582
8	Canada	477,468
9	Brazil	444,205
10	China	425,611
11	Mexico	343,472
12	Korea, Rep.	330,831
13	Russian Federation	329,432
14	Netherlands	309,227
15	Australia	289,390
16	Argentina	255,595
17	Switzerland	232,161
18	India	225,431
19	Belgium	210,576
20	Austria	182,067
21	Sweden	166,745
22	Turkey	156,413
23	Indonesia	144,707
24	**General Motors**	**133,622**
25	Thailand	124,862
26	Saudi Arabia	121,530
27	Denmark	117,587
28	Ukraine	109,078
29	**Ford Motor**	**108,521**
30	Iran, Islamic Rep.	107,335

31	South Africa	105,636
32	Norway	103,419
33	**Exxon**	**97,825**
34	**Royal Dutch/Shell**	**95,134**
35	Hong Kong	89,997
36	Poland	85,853
37	Portugal	85,665
38	**Toyota Motor**	**85,283**
39	Finland	74,124
40	Israel	69,739
41	**Hitachi**	**68,582**
42	Malaysia	64,450
43	**IBM**	**62,716**
44	**Matsushita Electric Ind.**	**61,385**
45	**General Electric**	**60,823**
46	Venezuela	59,995
47	**Daimler-Benz**	**59,102**
48	**Mobil**	**56,576**
49	Singapore	55,153
50	Colombia	54,076
51	Philippines	54,068
52	**Nissan Motor**	**53,760**
53	**British Petroleum**	**52,485**
54	**Samsung**	**51,345**
55	**Philip Morris**	**50,621**
56	**IRI**	**50,488**
57	**Siemens**	**50,381**
58	Pakistan	46,360
59	**Volkswagen**	**46,312**
60	New Zealand	43,699
61	Chile	43,684
62	**Chrysler**	**43,600**
63	Ireland	42,962
64	**Toshiba**	**42,917**
65	**Unilever**	**41,843**
66	Peru	41,061
67	Algeria	39,836

68	**Nestlé**	**38,894**
69	Hungary	38,099
70	**Elf Aquitaine**	**37,016**
71	Puerto Rico	35,834
72	**Honda Motor**	**35,798**
73	Egypt, Arab Rep.	35,784
74	United Arab Emirates	34,935
75	**ENI**	**34,791**
76	**Fiat**	**34,707**
77	**Sony**	**34,603**
78	**Texaco**	**34,359**
79	**NEC**	**33,176**
80	**Du Pont**	**32,621**
81	**Chevron**	**32,123**
82	**Philips Electronics**	**31,666**
83	Czech Republic	31,613
84	Nigeria	31,344
85	**Daewoo**	**30,893**
86	**Procter & Gamble**	**30,433**
87	**Renault**	**29,975**
88	**Fujitsu**	**29,094**
89	**Mitsubishi Electric**	**28,780**
90	**Abb Asea Browh Boveri**	**28,315**
91	**Hoechst**	**27,845**
92	**Alcatel Alsthom**	**27,599**
93	Belarus	27,545
94	**Mitsubishi Motors**	**27,311**
95	Morocco	26,635
96	**Pemex**	**26,573**
97	Romania	25,969
98	**Mitsubishi Heavy Ind.**	**25,804**
99	**Peugeot**	**25,669**
100	**Nippon Steel**	**25,481**

* Not included in this ranking are financial, trading, and retail companies. Sources: World Bank, *World Development Report 1996* (Oxford: Oxford University Press, 1995); *Fortune* "The World's Largest Industrial Corporations," July 25, 1994.

Appendix 2

Resources

Campaign for Global Change
World Federalist Association
418 7th Street SE
Washington, D.C. 20003
(800) 932-0123
Email: wfa@igc.apc.org

Campaign for UN Reform
713 D Street SE
Washington, D.C. 20003
(202) 546-3956
Contact: Eric Cox

Center for UN Reform Education
139 E. McClellan
Livingston, NJ 07039
(201) 994-1826
Contact: Myron Cornish

Centre for the Study of Global Governance
St. Philips Building
London School of Economics
Houghton Street
London WC2A 2AE
United Kingdom
(+071) 955-7583
Fax: (+071) 955-7591

Coalition for a Strong UN
2161 Massachusetts Avenue
Cambridge, MA 02141
(616) 576-3871
Contact: John Forbes

Global Policy Forum
P.O. Box 20022
New York, NY 10025
(212) 501-8134
Contact: Jim Paul
Email: globalpolicy@igc.apc.org

National Commission for Economic Conversion and Disarmament
1828 Jefferson Place NW
Washington, D.C. 20036
(202) 728-0815
Email: ncecd@igc.apc.org

Project on Peacekeeping and the United Nations
Council for a Livable World
Education Fund
110 Maryland Avenue, Suite 409
Washington, D.C. 20002
(202) 543-4100
Contact: Victoria Holt
Email: tholt@clw.org

Quaker United Nations Office
777 UN Plaza
New York, NY 10017
(212) 682-2745
Email: qunony@pipeline.com

Third World Network
228 MacAlister Road
10400 Penang
Malaysia
(+604) 229-3511
Email: twn@igc.apc.org

United Methodist Office for the United Nations
777 UN Plaza
New York, NY 10017-3585
(212) 682-3633
Contact: Mia Adjali

United Nations Association of the United States of America
485 Fifth Avenue
New York, NY 10017
(212) 967-3232

United Nations Department of Public Information
United Nations Plaza
New York, NY 10017
(212) 963-1234
WWW: http://www.un.org

United Nations Non-Governmental Liaison Service
866 United Nations Plaza
Room 6015
New York, NY 10017
(212) 963-3125
Email: ngls@igc.apc.org *or*
ngls@nywork2.undp.org

United States Mission to the United Nations
799 United Nations Plaza
New York, NY 10017-3505
(212) 415-4000

We the Peoples...
UN50 Committee
555 California Street, 28th Floor
San Francisco, CA 94104
(415) 989-1995
Email: un50@igc.apc.org

Index

national sovereignty xv, 5-6, 80, 83-85,
91, 155, 158-159
Netherlands 24
New International Economic Order
(NIEO) 10, 27, 64, 117-118, 120
New Zealand 150
Nicaragua 25, 50, 56-57, 134, 168
Nigeria 90, 150
Nixon, Richard 95
nongovernmental organizations (NGOs)
xvi, 27, 37-40, 123, 147, 156, 158,
165
Non-Proliferation Treaty (NPT) 26, 132
North American Free Trade Agreement
(NAFTA) 116
North Atlantic Treaty Organization (NATO)
78, 88-90, 96, 111-113
North Korea 30, 56, 78-80, 89, 132
North-South conflict 1, 152, 165; see also
the South
nuclear weapons 30, 56, 132; see also
Non-Proliferation Treaty

O

Ogata, Sadako 33
Organization of African Unity (OAU) 90,
108
Organization of American States (OAS)
89-90, 96, 105

P

Pakistan 30, 108, 132, 150
Palau 23
Palestine 79-80, 168
Palestine Liberation Organization (PLO)
25, 59
Panama 48, 51, 56, 90, 105, 168
Paying 60, 137, 139, 141, 168
Payment 60, 141
PDD-25 52-55, 96
peace operations 25, 49, 51-55, 60, 70-
71, 75-81, 84, 86-87, 89, 92-94, 96,
99-101, 103, 105, 107, 109-111, 113,
137-138, 151, 161-162
peacekeeping 1, 3, 17-20, 44, 50, 52-55,
60-62, 69-81, 86-89, 91-92, 95-97, 99-
101, 103, 105-107, 109-110, 112-113,
137, 139-140, 155, 157, 159-163, 167
Peacekeeping Reserve Fund 92
Pentagon 55, 61, 135
Persian Gulf War 48, 51-52, 66, 71, 89,
134

Portugal 99, 150
Pot, Pol 94, 103
Puerto Rico 45

R

Reagan, Ronald 25, 27, 46, 50, 56, 59-
60, 64, 144
refugees xvi, 33, 71, 87-88, 105-106
Rhodesia 80
Roosevelt, Franklin D. xv, 37, 43
Russia 14, 24, 55, 57, 89, 103, 111, 138,
140, 149, 159
Rwanda 33, 54, 88-89, 95, 166

S

Sakhnoun, Mohammad 108
sanctions 11, 56-57, 71, 106, 112, 160,
162-164
Saouma, Edouward 29
Saudi Arabia 134
Savimbi, Jonas 99-100
Security Council 1, 10-15, 17-22, 26, 38-
39, 45, 55, 57-58, 69-71, 75-77, 79-80,
84-85, 88-89, 92, 94, 96, 101, 103-104,
108, 110, 131-133, 139, 143, 146-152,
155, 157-158, 160-161, 167
Sen, Hun 101
Serbia 112, 140
Sinai 79
Singapore 84
Slovenia 111
Somalia 107, 110
South, the 14, 18, 49, 59, 124-125, 148;
see also North-South conflict
South Africa 83, 140, 150
South Korea 79
Southeast Asia 103
Soviet Union xiii, xv, 11, 14-15, 29, 44-
46, 51, 60, 66, 74-75, 79, 85, 90, 94,
100, 103, 107, 132, 148-149, 167
Spain 138
Stalin, Josef xv
State Department (U.S.) 38
Stockholm 26
Sudan 86
Suez conflict 17
sustainable development 10, 26-27, 40,
121
South West Africa People's Organization
(SWAPO) 59

T

Taiwan 11

Tajikistan 89
Thornburgh, Richard 121, 139
Tiananmen Square massacre 58
Transnational Corporations (TNCs) 23, 27, 67, 115, 117-121, 127, 156, 167
Trusteeship Council 10, 23
Turkey 85, 134

U

Ukraine 140
UN Children's Fund (UNICEF) 34-36, 122, 134, 166
UN Conference on Trade and Development (UNCTAD) 61, 117-118, 120
UN Development Program (UNDP) 33-35, 118, 122
UN High Commissioner for Refugees (UNHCR) 33, 44
UN Industrial Development Organization (UNIDO) 61, 117-118
UNITA 99-100
United Nations: arrears 55, 59-61, 92, 121, 139-141, 168; budget 21, 26, 59-60, 92, 96, 137-139, 141, 145, 149; bureaucracy 20, 22, 92, 124; Charter 4-6, 10-11, 13, 15, 37-39, 76-77, 83, 90, 96, 116, 150, 152, 162, 165; democracy in 144; peace operations 51-53, 55, 60, 71, 77, 79-80, 84, 86-87, 92-94, 96, 99-100, 138, 162; Secretariat 19, 88, 96, 138, 140; secretary-general 10, 19-21, 26, 77, 88, 121, 123, 126, 137, 143, 162, 167; surrogates 89; system 9-10, 18-22, 24, 26-27, 29, 31, 33, 35, 39, 61-62, 125, 141, 143, 146
United States: government 5, 27, 34-35, 50, 52, 59-63, 81, 106, 121, 134, 144, 152, 168; hegemony of 44, 49-50, 65-66, 94; non-payment of UN dues 60; permanent representative 45; role in UN 43, 45, 47, 49, 51-53, 55, 57, 59, 61, 63, 65, 67, 167; use of veto by 56-57
UN Non-governmental Liaison Service (NGLS) 39
UN Population Fund (UNFPA) 28, 59
UN Transitional Authority in Cambodia (UNTAC) 102-103
Uzbekistan 140

V

Versailles Peace Conference 2
Versailles Treaty 24, 30
Vietnam 45, 50, 94, 101-103
Vietnam War 69

W

Warsaw Pact 90
West Bank 56
Western Sahara 56, 86
Wilson, Woodrow 2-3, 43
World Bank 19-20, 22, 27, 29-32, 34-35, 44, 58, 115, 120, 122, 124, 126-127, 137, 139, 144, 165
World Health Organization (WHO) 36, 124
World Trade Organization (WTO) 27, 29, 115, 120, 126, 144, 165
World War I 2-3, 62
World War II xiv, 3-4, 11, 23, 35, 37-38, 43, 49-50, 62, 69, 76, 81, 115, 149, 161

Y

Yeltsin, Boris 14
Yemen 58
Yugoslavia 33, 52, 64, 70, 74, 86, 88-89, 94-95, 100, 110-113, 134, 140, 166

Z

Zaire 58

The Resource Center

The Interhemispheric Resource Center is a private, nonprofit, research and policy institute located in New Mexico. Founded in 1979, the Resource Center produces books, policy reports, and other educational materials about U.S. foreign policy, as well as sponsoring popular education projects. For more information and a catalog of publications, please write to the Resource Center, Box 4506, Albuquerque, New Mexico 87196.

Board of Directors

ZAPATA'S REVENGE

Free Trade and the Farm Crisis in Mexico
by Tom Barry

The past and future collide in this compelling account of the drama unfolding in the Mexican countryside. Visions of a modernized and industrialized nation competing in the global market clash with the sobering reality of a desperate peasantry and falling agricultural production. These crises in Chiapas are the same ones confronting most of Mexico and the third world.

Barry views the crisis that confronts Mexico as alarming evidence of the incapacity of today's neoliberal and free trade policies to foster broad economic development. He explains that such strategies have resulted in reduced food security, environmental destruction, increased rural-urban polarization, depopulation of peasant communities and social and political instability.

This book offers personal interviews, investigative research, and analysis that goes to the heart of the development challenge faced by Mexico and other Latin American nations.

South End Press, 1995
ISBN 089608-499-X

250 PAGES
$16.00 paper

$35.00